*The Current Negotiations in the WTO:*
*Options, Opportunities and Risks for Developing Countries*
is published by

Third World Network
131 Jalan Macalister
10400 Penang, Malaysia

and

Zed Books Ltd
7 Cynthia Street
London, N1 9JF, UK
and Room 400, 175 Fifth Avenue
New York, NY 10010, USA.
www.zedbooks.co.uk

Distributed in the USA exclusively by
Palgrave Macmillan
a division of St Martin's Press, LLC
175 Fifth Avenue
New York, NY 10010, USA.



First edition: 2005
Second edition: 2007

Printed by Jutaprint
2, Solok Sungei Pinang 3, Sg. Pinang
11600 Penang, Malaysia.



ISBN 978-1-84277-923-1 hb (Zed Books)
ISBN 978-1-84277-924-8 pb (Zed Books)
ISBN 978-983-2729-78-5 (TWN)

A catalogue record for this book is available from the British Library.
US CIP data is available from the Library of Congress.

In memory

of

***Shreemati Chandra Das***

*Previous books by the same author*
*(co-published by Third World Network and Zed Books)*

An Introduction to the WTO Agreements

The WTO Agreements: Deficiencies, Imbalances and Required Changes

The World Trade Organisation: A Guide to the Framework for International Trade

WTO: The Doha Agenda – The New Negotiations on World Trade

The WTO and the Multilateral Trading System: Past, Present and Future

# CONTENTS

# PREFACE TO 2005 EDITION

THE member countries of the World Trade Organization (WTO) have been engaging in comprehensive multilateral trade negotiations since the WTO's Doha Ministerial Conference in November 2001. The negotiations suffered a serious setback in the Cancun Ministerial Conference in September 2003, but were revived by an agreement in the WTO General Council at the end of July 2004. The negotiations are expected to gain momentum during the course of 2005, as there will certainly be pressure to bring some concrete results to the next Ministerial Conference, to be held in Hong Kong in December 2005. It is feared that the developing countries will remain under pressure throughout the course of these negotiations.

Of course, they also have the opportunity to correct the wrongs done to them during the previous Uruguay Round of negotiations. But whether and to what extent they will succeed in doing so will depend a lot on their technical preparations and political cohesion. The opportunity to correct the imbalances and inequities in the WTO agreements will not come again for a very long time. Hence this opportunity should not be missed. It will be helpful if the developing countries change their mood of diffidence and frustration to one of confidence and strength.

They have been denied their rights of export in the textiles and some other sectors for the last three to four decades and then pressurized into curtailing their rights in services sectors and intellectual property over the last 10 years in favour of the major developed countries. The latter, for their part, have refused to eliminate their agricultural subsidies that expose the farmers of the developing countries to grave risks of loss of livelihood. They have also resisted lowering their much-higher-than-average tariffs on industrial products that harm the export prospects of the developing countries.

This unfair and iniquitous state of affairs in international economic relations must not be allowed to continue. But it cannot be redressed by meek submission to the loud demands and bullying tactics of the major developed countries, propelled by their powerful economic entities. Strong political will is needed on the part of the developing countries, backed by sound technical expertise.

This book is a modest attempt at contributing to the technical input that is so much needed by the developing countries' negotiators and policymakers. It brings out the wide range of options which the developing countries still have within the framework of the ongoing trade negotiations and makes suggestions for using this to their advantage.

The materials and discussions contained in the book have been set in the context of the current negotiations, but they may have a continuing relevance that extends beyond these, as the problems will not all vanish with the end of these negotiations even with the best of efforts. Moreover, the range of options given in the book may also help in the assessment of the final outcome of the negotiations based on where the outcome is located within this spectrum of options. For the present, if this work encourages the developing countries to choose the options suitable to them and pursue these options in the negotiations, it would have amply served its purpose.

Several persons have played a role in this effort. Martin Khor of the Third World Network has been a constant source of encouragement and support. Lean Ka-Min of the Third World Network edited the text, which has been vastly improved by his efforts. Abhijit Das undertook the exercise of reading the earlier version of the manuscript and made valuable suggestions which have been incorporated in the final text. Papers and documents obtained from the South Centre in Geneva and the Geneva office of the Third World Network helped me significantly in preparing the text. I express my most sincere thanks to them all.

**Bhagirath Lal Das**

# Chapter 1

# INTRODUCTION

THE World Trade Organization (WTO) has launched an ambitious programme of negotiations in its Doha Work Programme in accordance with the decisions of its Doha Ministerial Conference held in November 2001. After the Uruguay Round of multilateral trade negotiations (1986-1994), this is a major exercise in the GATT/WTO system.[1]

The initial time frame as set in Doha was to conclude the negotiations in three years, which was very ambitious, considering the complexity of the negotiations. Not surprisingly, there was very little progress up to the next WTO Ministerial Conference, held in Cancun in September 2003, which ended without any result on the issues involved in the negotiations. This failure in Cancun, after an almost similar failure in the Seattle Ministerial Conference in December 1999, resulted in a serious erosion of the credibility of the multilateral trading system. The main issues over which there were severe differences, viz., agriculture, non-agricultural market access (NAMA) and Singapore issues (investment, competition policy, transparency in government procurement and trade facilitation)[2], were followed up on in the General Council of the WTO and an agreement was reached at the end of July 2004.

After the severe setback at Cancun, the decision of the General Council of 1 August 2004 has brought the WTO negotiations back on track. Already technical discussions have started in various negotiating groups. However, the preliminary statements indicate that the way ahead is not smooth. The developing countries have to make special efforts to ensure that the negotiations are headed in a direction that can be beneficial to them. An attempt is made here to assist them in this exercise. Also, suggestions are put forward here to improve the negotiating environment in the WTO so that it is conducive to achieving results for the benefit of all groups of Members of the trade body.

The negotiations under the Doha Work Programme present both an opportunity and a risk for the developing countries. Herein lies an opportunity to rectify the inequities, imbalances and deficiencies in the current WTO agreements and also improve the implementation of the agreements. In addition, there is an opportunity to improve the decision-making process and negotiating environment in the WTO which has left the developing countries dismayed over the last 10 years of operation of the WTO.[3] Side by side, however, there is the risk that these new negotiations, as in the Uruguay Round, may instead impose still more onerous obligations on the developing countries and may further constrain their development options.

The Doha Ministerial Declaration of November 2001 (Doha Declaration) (reproduced in Annex 1 of this book) and the WTO General Council decision of 1 August 2004 (commonly referred to as the "July 2004 decision") (Annex 2) constitute the combined framework of the current negotiations. The former is supplemented by the latter in the areas of agriculture, NAMA and trade facilitation. Three of the Singapore issues, viz., investment, competition policy and transparency in government procurement, have been dropped from the Doha Work Programme by the July 04 decision.

The Doha Declaration prescribed only broad objectives for the agriculture and NAMA negotiations. The July 04 decision now prescribes specifics in terms of directions of commitments and alternative approaches to achieve the objectives. The renewed negotiations will thus be for choosing among the alternatives and including quantitative parameters in the commitments. Admittedly, the July 04 decision has been a significant move forward from the Doha Declaration in these two areas. The same is also true for trade facilitation, where the negotiations will now be on working out a multilateral agreement on this issue.

These and other important subjects in the Doha Declaration are covered in the various chapters that follow. For each subject, the framework of the negotiations is discussed first along with the implications. Then the proposals of the developing countries are analyzed and suggestions are given on what should be done. Chapter 12 discusses the critical issues that may prove to be the make-or-break issues in these negotiations, and Chapter 13 suggests ways to improve the negotiating environment in the WTO. Finally, Chapter 14 examines the potential substantive and procedural pitfalls the developing countries should avoid in the talks if they are to secure negotiating outcomes which best advance their interests.

# Chapter 2

# AGRICULTURE

## FRAMEWORK[4]

ANNEX A to the July 04 decision (Annex A) provides the operative framework for further negotiations on agriculture and talks have already started on that basis. Two "balancing" objectives have been stipulated in it (the paragraph references in this chapter on agriculture point to the paragraph numbers in Annex A, except if otherwise specified):

(i) balance between the results in agriculture and other areas covered by the single undertaking in the Doha Declaration (para 2); and
(ii) balance in the results among the three pillars of the agriculture negotiations, viz., export subsidies, domestic support and market access (para 3).

In addition, balancing, through the concept of "parallelism" (i.e., equal or equivalent commitments as well as similar pace of implementation), is envisaged within the pillar of export subsidies itself:

(i) between commitments on direct subsidies and those on other measures with equivalent effects, e.g., export credits, credit guarantees and insurance programmes (para 17); and
(ii) in commitments by Members in respect of elimination/reduction of subsidies and equivalent measures (para 21).

The first implies a balance between the possible commitments of the European Union (EU) and the United States (US), as the former mostly uses direct subsidies and the latter mostly uses other measures. The second implies a balance in the overall commitments of Members in the specific area of export subsidies in agriculture. This contrasts with the usual feature of multilateral trade negotiations where balance is normally considered by taking obligations in all areas together and not in any specific area (e.g., only agriculture) or sub-area (e.g., only export subsidies in agriculture) as in this case.

### Commonly used terms in the agriculture negotiations

For this chapter on agriculture, an explanation of some colour-code terms used in the negotiations on domestic support/subsidies is necessary for clarity, as these terms will be frequently used:

**"Amber Box" subsidies**: the domestic subsidies covered by Article 6.2 of the WTO Agreement on Agriculture (AoA), technically called the Aggregate Measurement of Support (AMS) and measured mainly in terms of the difference between the domestic price and the international price. These are subject to reduction under the AoA.

**"Blue Box" subsidies**: the domestic subsidies covered by Article 6.5 of the AoA. These are direct payments to producers based on area/yield and not subject to reduction in the AoA. They are largely used by the EU.

**"Green Box" subsidies**: the domestic subsidies covered by Annex 2 of the AoA. These include various types of direct payments to producers, including income support not related to volume of production or price. It is claimed that such payments are not trade-distorting and they are not subject to reduction in the AoA. But, as will be explained later, they do have the effect of distorting trade and production. Such subsidies are used in a big way by both the US and the EU.

This colour-code nomenclature is not employed in the AoA itself. Instead, these were common and popular appellations adopted at some stages in the course of the Uruguay Round negotiations and have continued in common use.

Also, the AoA always refers to domestic subsidies as "domestic support", presumably in an attempt to distance them from subsidies that distort trade and production. But, as will be explained later, all these three forms of "domestic support" (i.e., Amber Box, Blue Box and Green Box) actually amount to subsidies. In the analysis and discussion here, the terms "domestic support" and "domestic subsidy" are used interchangeably.

The main elements of the framework for the agriculture negotiations are as follows:

**Export subsidies**: Export subsidies and equivalent measures like export credits, export credit guarantees and insurance programmes with repayment periods beyond 180 days are to be eliminated by a date to be fixed. Such measures with lesser repayment periods are to be brought under agreed disciplines or are to be eliminated by the fixed date. Trade-distorting practices related to state trading enterprises (e.g., subsidies given to them or by them, government financing, underwriting of losses, etc.) are to be eliminated by the fixed date. The provision of food aid is to be brought under agreed disciplines or eliminated by the fixed date (para 18).

**Domestic support:** Reduction is first envisaged for the total "trade-distorting" support, which is specified as the sum of three elements, viz., (i) the Aggregate Measurement of Support (AMS), i.e., "Amber Box" subsidies; (ii) the *de minimis* support, which, in the case of the developed countries, for product-specific support is 5 percent of the production of that product, plus, in the case of non-product-specific support, 5 percent of total agricultural production (10 percent in the case of the developing countries for each); and (iii) the support under Article 6.5 of the AoA, i.e., "Blue Box" subsidies. All these, taken together, will be "substantially" reduced (para 6). As the first instalment of the cut, the total of these three elements will not exceed 80 percent of the base level; thus the minimum cut will be 20 percent in the beginning (para 7).

Then separate disciplines for reduction/capping are further envisaged for the AMS (Amber Box), *de minimis* and Blue Box. The AMS will be reduced "substantially" using a tiered approach in which Members having higher total AMS will make greater reductions (para 9). *De minimis* support will be reduced as negotiated (para 11). Blue Box subsidies will not exceed 5 percent of the agricultural production of a Member (para 15) and can be used by Members in accordance with the criteria to be negotiated (para 14).

The criteria for Annex 2 ("Green Box") subsidies will be reviewed and clarified so as to ensure that these subsidies have no, or at most minimal, trade-distorting effects or effects on production (para 16).

**Market access:** There will be a tiered formula for tariff reduction with the objective of "substantial overall tariff reduction and substantial trade expansion". There will be deeper cuts in higher tariffs (paras 28, 29). For the tiered formula, the formation of bands and reduction of tariff in each band will be negotiated (para 30). (A tariff band contains products with existing tariffs within a given range. For example, there may be a band with products having current tariffs in the 0-10% range, another band for tariff range 11-50%, and so on.) Members may designate some "sensitive products" which will be treated differently. Here substantial improvement in market access will be achieved through a combination of tariff reductions and tariff rate quotas (TRQ) (paras 31, 32, 33). The formula for addressing tariff escalation will be negotiated (para 36). The future of the Special Safeguard (SSG), used mainly by the developed countries, will be negotiated (para 38).

In consideration of their rural-development, food-security and livelihood-security needs, the developing countries will be accorded special and differential treatment in respect of tariff reduction, sensitive products, TRQ and implementation period (paras 39, 40). These countries may designate some products as Special Products (SP) which will have more flexible treatment. The criteria for selection as SP and the flexible treatment for such products will be specified further in the negotiations (para 41). A Special Safeguard Mechanism (SSM) to be used by the developing countries will be established (para 42). The fullest liberalization of trade in tropical products and those for diversification from illicit narcotic crops will be addressed effectively in the negotiations (para 43).

The least developed countries (LDCs) are not required to undertake reduction commitments. Further, developed countries and developing countries in a position to do so "should" provide duty-free and quota-free market access for products originating in LDCs (para 45).

## RANGE OF OPTIONS

The simple exposition above does not bring to light the immense technical complexities and political frictions underlying the framework. Almost every clear and specific action prescribed in the framework has a balancing counter-stipulation, indicating the precarious balance of interests in this framework.

The framework leaves open a wide range of options in each area of the agriculture negotiations, which presents both a risk and an opportunity for the developing countries. One end of the range in various areas will be most favourable to the developing countries, while the other end will likely be most adverse. These extremes are given below. The final negotiated position in each area will likely be somewhere between these extremes. Its exact location within the range will determine the extent to which it is favourable or adverse to the developing countries. Given such a range of options, the future course and final result will depend a lot on the preparation and strength of the participants in the negotiations.

The developing countries, individually, in groups and as a whole, will naturally be working out what points in this spectrum of choices indicated below are in their interest. The objective in indicating the two extremes in each area is to alert the developing countries to the opportunities and risks involved. A subsequent section in this chapter will suggest some preferred options within these ranges.

## *EXPORT SUBSIDIES*[5]

(i) The direct subsidies and equivalent measures with repayment periods of more than 180 days may be eliminated at an early date.

Or

The date of final elimination may be fixed in the distant future.

(ii) The equivalent measures with shorter repayment periods may be subjected to hard disciplines, with the result that most of them will have to be terminated by the fixed date.

Or

The disciplines may be soft, allowing them to continue indefinitely.

(iii) Disciplines on food aid may be strict, thus requiring elimination of most of the current types of food aid.

Or

The disciplines may be soft, thus letting most of it continue indefinitely.

(iv) The process of implementation of elimination/reduction will be by "annual instalments" (para 20). There is no guideline about the size of the instalments. Thus the initial instalments could be large, leaving only small instalments for the later years, which would mean quicker elimination/reduction.

Or

The initial instalments could be small, thus delaying the process of elimination/reduction.

The only guideline for the termination date in the framework is that it should be "credible" (para 17). This suggests that the end date should not be fixed too far in the future, because that would erode the credibility of the objective of "establish(ing) a fair and market-oriented trading system" (para 1). At the same time, it is a rather weak and defensive formulation, as it falls far short of asking for "immediate" or even "quick" elimination.

The stipulation of annual instalments indicates that the time frame is expected to be longer than one year.

Also, the "credible" date is circumscribed by stipulating that the "phasing (of export subsidies and equivalents) will take into account the need for some coherence with internal reform steps of Members" (para 20). This appears to be a reference to the EU internal reform process where some of the export subsidies are currently envisaged to continue for a long time, even up to 2013 in certain cases. However, the "coherence" sought here is not mandatory; it only has to be taken into account. Hence there is no commitment at present to abide by the internal reform steps of individual Members and thus even such Members that are engaged in internal reform may be called upon to eliminate their export subsidies earlier.

The guideline for disciplines on food aid is that their objective is to "prevent commercial displacement" (para 18). It has a vital link with the current practice, mainly of the US, of disposing of excess food production in the form of food aid. The food is given to developing-country governments and US organizations which then sell it in the target country at low prices. Such "aid" may not be related to the existence of any disaster situation in that country or its actual needs. In effect, such food aid may result in commercial displacement in the food market in these target countries.

### *DOMESTIC SUPPORT*

(i) The sum of "trade-distorting support", i.e., AMS, *de minimis* and Blue Box subsidies, may be kept at 80 percent of the base level in all the years of the implementation period (para 7).[6]

Or

It may be kept at 80 percent in the first year of the implementation period, and be further reduced in subsequent years.

Or

It may start at a much lower level in the first year (80 percent is stipulated as the maximum level, thus lower levels are possible; no lowest limit is prescribed) and then either continue at that level or be further reduced in the subsequent years of the implementation period.

(ii) In the tiered reduction of the AMS, i.e., greater reduction in higher AMS, the formula may be such that most of the AMS is subjected to the highest reduction rate and the reduction rate is itself very steep.[7]

Or

Most of the AMS is covered by only a marginal reduction. (One can have graded reductions, all of them small.)

(iii) The *de minimis* subsidies for the developed countries may be kept at near zero (para 11).

Or

They may be reduced but kept near the current level.

(iv) The *de minimis* subsidies for the developing countries that are not meant for subsistence and resource-poor farmers may be kept at near zero (para 11). (Those meant for subsistence and resource-poor farmers will be exempt from reduction.)[8]

Or

They may be reduced but kept near the current level.

(v) Present high levels of Blue Box subsidies (particularly in the case of the EU) may be required to be cut by only a small amount, as flexibility is to be provided to a Member which has "placed an exceptionally large percentage of its trade-distorting support in the Blue Box" to ensure that the Member is not required to "make a wholly disproportionate cut" (para 15).

Or

The Blue Box support may be restricted to 5 percent of total agricultural production.

Or

The Blue Box support may be kept at a level much lower than 5 percent of production, as 5 percent is stipulated as the ceiling and not the norm, thus making lower levels possible.

(vi) The Blue Box subsidies could be extended for use even by Members who did not use them in any substantial manner in the past, for example the US (paras 13, 15).

Or

The criteria for the Blue Box may be set in such a manner that it is not applied by new Members and its use is fully/substantially restricted even for Members using it at present, for example the EU. The entire criteria for the Blue Box are to be negotiated, hence it is a totally open situation (para 14).

(vii) The criteria for the Green Box subsidies may be so strict as to make most of the present subsidies inadmissible. The criteria for the Green Box are to be reviewed and clarified, hence the situation is very much open (para 16).

Or

The criteria may be so fixed as to allow the present Green Box subsidies and even allow some new ones.

Or

The criteria may be fixed so that only the subsidies for retirement of resources from agriculture and for meeting emergency situations like epidemics or sudden crop failure are allowed and others expressly prohibited.

## *MARKET ACCESS*

(i) In the tiered approach for reduction of tariffs, i.e., deeper cuts for higher tariffs, there may be separate sets of bands for the developed countries and the developing countries (paras 27, 28, 30).

Or

There may be same sets of bands for the developing countries and developed countries. Though the criteria for the formation of bands have not been defined and the manner of tariff cuts within different bands has not been specified, it has been stipulated that special and differential treatment will be an integral part of all elements in the negotiations (para 27) and different tariff structures of the developed countries and developing countries will be taken into account (para 28).

(ii) There may be separate methods of tariff reduction within the bands for the developing countries and the developed countries. For example, there may be a set formula for the developed countries, whereas the developing countries may not be guided by any set formula for specific tariff lines (para 27, 28, 30). All these are subject to negotiations and special and differential treatment of developing countries will be an integral part of the negotiations.

Or

There may be a same or similar formula for both the developed countries and the developing countries.

(iii) The developing countries may only be required to reduce their average tariff by a certain percentage, as was the case in the Uruguay Round and as has been advocated by the developing countries (para 30).

Or

The developing countries may be required to follow a more onerous course of adopting the "Swiss formula" for tariff reduction that will result in deep cuts in individual tariff lines, as has been advocated by some major developed countries. All this is still open for negotiations (para 30).

(iv) The tariff peaks and high tariffs in the developed countries may be substantially reduced (para 30).

Or

The tariff peaks and high tariffs in the developed countries may continue, with marginal reductions. The process of tariff caps will be the subject of further consideration (para 30).

(v) The developed countries may be allowed to designate a large number of products as sensitive products, and tariff reduction in these cases, though substantial (para 32), may still be comparatively small. The designation of sensitive products is to be negotiated and their treatment is to be considered further (paras 31, 33).

Or

The sensitive products of the developed countries may be very much limited in number and the tariff reduction, though lower, may still be substantial.

(vi) Tariff escalation in the developed countries may be totally abolished (para 36), as has been the demand of the developing countries.

Or

It may only get marginal treatment. This subject is to be addressed through a formula to be negotiated and agreed (para 36).

(vii) The Special Safeguard (SSG), which can only be used primarily by the developed countries and a very limited number of developing countries, may be abolished (para 38).

Or

The SSG may continue in the present manner. It is under negotiation.

(viii) A developing country may itself designate some products as Special Products based on its food-security, livelihood-security and rural-development needs. Also, the treatment of these products may ensure wide flexibility for the protection of domestic production of these products and assurance for their market-access opportunities abroad (para 41).[9]

Or

The criteria set for selection of Special Products may limit such products to a small number. Also, these products may get only marginal flexibility. The criteria and treatment of these products are to be further specified during the negotiations (para 41).

(ix) It is agreed that a Special Safeguard Mechanism (SSM) will be established for use by the developing countries. The criteria for triggering the SSM, the nature of the measures and the procedures may be such that the developing countries may be able to use the SSM effectively and easily (para 42).

Or

The trigger and the procedures may be so restrictive that the use of the SSM may be highly limited. Establishment of the SSM is agreed, but the criteria for triggering it, the nature of the measures to be taken under it and the procedures are to be negotiated (para 42).

## COORDINATED POSITIONS OF DEVELOPED COUNTRIES

Most of the agreed points in the framework appear to have emerged essentially out of compromises among the major developed countries, particularly the US and the EU. They appear to have mutually settled many of the issues, providing concessions to each other and accommodating the interests of each other.

For example, in the area of **export subsidies**, the US seems to have persuaded the EU to fix an end date for eliminating direct subsidies; and the EU, in turn, appears to have persuaded the US to include other equivalent measures and food aid in the elimination process. This should be seen in the background of the currently prevailing situation. While the EU uses high levels of direct export subsidies, the US mainly uses equivalent measures and food aid. The positive side of this development for the developing countries is that both the direct subsidies and the equivalent measures, including food aid, will be eliminated by an end date/put under strict discipline. The negative side is that the US and the EU together may adopt the principle of "mutual forgiveness" and continue with a substantial part of their respective subsidies and measures for a long time to come.

In the area of **domestic support**, the US seems to have agreed to tolerate the Blue Box subsidies of the EU to a great extent. And the EU, in turn, seems to have agreed to the expansion of the scope of the Blue Box so that the US may also use it. The result is that the developing countries will now be afflicted by the Blue Box subsidies of both the US and the EU. This development should be seen in the context of the recent practices of the US and the EU. The EU has been the main user of the Blue Box. A bilateral understanding between the US and the EU towards the end of the Uruguay Round resulted in the relevant provision (Article 6.5 of the AoA) whereby the EU was allowed to use it. But it was frowned upon by the other countries. The US eliminated its Blue Box subsidies in 1996. The general expectation was that the EU too would eliminate it in the near future. But the situation took a sudden turn in 1998 when the US again started with this type of payment. Then it included such payments in its Farm Bill of 2002. Thus both the US and the EU now have a stake in its future continuance. The reason the US is keen to expand the coverage of the Blue Box is that its recent provisions for payments cannot be covered by the Green Box. These are counter-cyclical payments related to price, whereas the relevant Green Box provision for income support in paragraph 6 of Annex 2 to the AoA states that such support has to be unrelated to price.

In the area of **market access** too, the major developed countries have combined to include a possibility of drastic tariff reduction in the developing countries, as has been explained above. Thus the developing countries have been put somewhat on the defensive.

Further, the interests of the US, the EU and many other developed countries have been taken into account by providing for the sensitive-products category that was mainly their demand. This may enable them to continue to keep high tariffs on some of their products.

The forging of a common and combined position by the major developed countries poses a grave challenge to the developing countries. They will be under great pressure to open their markets to the products of the major developed countries, even as the major developed countries themselves continue comfortably with their high subsidies and high tariffs on some products of interest to them.

It is in this background of the new framework of the negotiations and possible combined pressure from the major developed countries that we now examine the proposals of the developing countries.

## DEVELOPING COUNTRIES' PROPOSALS

The developing countries have given their proposals in various forms: as specific proposals in formal papers, as amendments to or comments on Chairman's texts, as statements, etc. Though somewhat cumbersome, it is useful to list some of the detailed proposals here. These include the proposals put forward by the Group of 20 (G20) in WTO document WT/MIN(03)/W/6 of 4 September 2003; by some members of what later came to be known as the G33 in JOB(03)/59 of 20 March 2003; by the G33 in JOB(04)/65 of 1 June 2004; by the Dominican Republic, Honduras, Nicaragua and Panama in WT/MIN(03)/W/10 of 5 September 2003; by Kenya in JOB(03)/175 of 25 August 2003; and by the Africa Group in JOB(02)/187 of 20 November 2002 and also in G/AG/NG/W/142 of 23 March 2001. Also, there are proposals in the form of comments from some countries on the Chairman's text of 16 July 2004. Some of the detailed ones are by the G20, the Africa Group, Jamaica-Barbados-Trinidad and Tobago, the African, Caribbean and Pacific (ACP) Group, the LDCs, the G33 and Jamaica.

### *EXPORT SUBSIDIES*

These proposals ask for the elimination of the developed countries' export subsidies by a definite date to be fixed. Some of them ask for an earlier date in the case of products of export interest to the developing countries and "fast-track" elimination for products of export interest to the LDCs.

They also ask for disciplines on equivalent measures and elimination of the subsidy component in them, as well as disciplines to prevent commercial displacement through food aid.

The proposals of the Africa Group, the ACP Group and Kenya add that the process of elimination and disciplines on the equivalent measures and food aid should take into account the conditions, needs, concerns and negative effects on the LDCs and net food-importing developing countries (NFIDCs).

Article 9.4 (on exemption of developing countries' subsidies for handling, upgrading, international transport, etc. and for additional cost in internal transport of export products over domestic trade) and Article 12 (on exemption of developing countries from disciplines on export prohibition on foodstuff) of the AoA should be continued. The G20 proposal mentions the former but misses the latter.

The state trading enterprises of the developing countries should be exempted from the disciplines to be evolved.

## *DOMESTIC SUPPORT*

The developing countries' proposals call for deep cuts, in a tiered way, in the Amber Box subsidies. Subsidies which have been applied to products for a long time should be subjected to upper levels of reduction. Also, subsidies on products having a share in world exports beyond a given limit are required to be subjected to upper levels of reduction and gradually eliminated.

The *de minimis* subsidies of the developed countries are sought to be eliminated or sharply reduced.

The Blue Box subsidies are sought to be eliminated or significantly reduced. The expansion of the scope for these subsidies, which has been put forward as an option in the framework, is opposed. It has been asserted that any such expansion will undermine the reform process that is the objective of the Doha Work Programme. Entitlement for trade-distorting subsidies should be reduced; it must not be increased. It is feared that extension of the Blue Box to cover new situations will work as a loophole allowing for enhanced subsidies.

For Green Box subsidies, disciplines are to be elaborated and these subsidies are to be capped/reduced. There should be a review of the trade-distorting elements of these subsidies. The Africa Group proposal adds that the Green Box subsidies covered by paragraphs 5, 6 and 7 of Annex 2 of the AoA should be transferred to the Amber Box and subjected to reduction discipline. Further, there should be criteria in terms of the level of loss of production for entitlement to disaster relief under the Green Box.

As special and differential treatment, the subsidies of the developing countries allowed in Article 6.2 of the AoA should be continued and expanded, and they should be applicable whether or not they are targeted to specific categories of producers and products. (At present, they are normally to be targeted to low-income and resource-poor farmers.) The permissible level of *de minimis* subsidies for the developing countries should continue. Kenya's proposal also asks for the rolling over of the unutilized portion of it to the next year.

## *MARKET ACCESS*

The developed countries should have some percentages of tariff lines subjected respectively to a specified percentage of tariff cut, Swiss formula cut and zero duty. There should be a ceiling on their tariff levels. Tariff rate quotas should be expanded by a certain percentage of domestic consumption. There should be zero duty on tropical products and on other products representing a certain percentage of imports from the developing countries. The Special Safeguard for the developed countries should be discontinued. The sensitive products should be limited in number and should not be exempted from the disciplines of the bands; whatever consideration they receive should be within the respective bands. Merely following the TRQ route should not be enough for them. Non-tariff barriers (NTBs) should be effectively addressed along with tariff reduction in the negotiations.

The LDCs should be exempted from any tariff reduction. The other developing countries should reduce their average tariffs by a certain percentage, with a certain percentage of minimum cut, but without any obligation to apply any formula for individual tariffs. They should not be required to have any expansion of tariff rate quotas and reduction of in-quota tariffs. There should be provisions on Special Products for the developing countries having regard to their food-security, livelihood-security and rural-development needs. There should be a Special Safeguard Mechanism for the developing countries. The question of erosion of tariff preferences should be addressed.

The provisions on sensitive products and Special Products are based on entirely different considerations. Thus they should not be mixed up in treatment and must not be linked in any way.

There are certain variations of emphasis in different proposals on some points. For example, for tackling tariff escalation, there is a proposal that the reduction rate for processed products should have a multiplier. Another proposal says that the rate of reduction for the processed product should be equivalent to that for the primary product.

Similarly, for special and differential treatment of the developing countries, some proposals specify that in case the developing countries are to reduce the average tariff, the reduction should not be more than 50 percent of that to be undertaken by the developed countries. For Special Products, some proposals, particularly those of Kenya, Dominican Republic et al., the G33 and the Africa Group, specify that the designation of these products applicable to a developing country should be done by the country itself. There could be a limit on the number of Special Products by specifying that it should not exceed a certain percentage of the total number of products. These proposals specify that the Special Products should be exempted from tariff reduction and also that the SSM should be applicable to them.

On the erosion of preferences, the Africa Group proposal says that there should be minimum economic cost of erosion and there should be a holistic approach in coordination with other international institutions. The proposal also gives details of the process of TRQ expansion and also of criteria and procedures for the SSM. It further suggests that the implementation of the commitments of the developing countries (of Africa) should be postponed until the export subsidies and domestic support of the developed countries have been totally eliminated.

## *PROPOSALS IN HARMONY*

There is no basic difference among the various proposals of the developing countries, although sometimes there may be differences in emphasis and thrust. Also, some of the proposals may complement the others. The proposals generally appear to be mutually harmonious, while some of them contain some additional provisions compared to the others. There is no mutual contradiction at all; hence it should be possible for the developing countries to work out a common and unified approach to the negotiations which will add significantly to their negotiating strength and capacity. We consider now some of the additions and complementary points in the three pillars of the negotiations.

On export subsidies, while all the proposals call for the elimination of the developed countries' export subsidies and disciplines on equivalent measures and food aid, an added stipulation in the proposals of Kenya, the Africa Group and the ACP Group is that the negative effects on the LDCs and NFIDCs should be taken into account.

On domestic support, the proposals call for elimination/substantial reduction of the Amber Box subsidies, Blue Box subsidies and *de minimis* subsidies as well as capping/disciplining the Green Box subsidies of the developed countries. The provision of Article 6.2 of the AoA exempting some subsidies of the developing countries from reduction should be expanded and the *de minimis* level for the developing countries should be retained. Some of the proposals are more specific on some of these points. Nevertheless, the main points and thrust of the proposals are quite harmonious and mutually aligned.

On market access, the proposals seek a substantial reduction of tariffs in the developed countries by the use of part simple reduction, part Swiss-formula application and part zero tariff. Sensitive products are to be limited in number and treatment. Tariff escalation is to be eliminated/reduced by higher reduction rates for processed products. Tariff peaks are to be reduced to a ceiling level. The SSG is to be discontinued. NTBs should be effectively addressed. The developing countries should undertake a reduction in their average tariff level but without any requirement to apply any formula for specific tariff lines. They should select the Special Products themselves within some limits on their number. The SSM should be established for their use. The proposals of Kenya, the Africa Group and the ACP Group ask for a mechanism for addressing the erosion of preferences.

The proposals of the developing countries in this area are also generally harmonized and aligned, although some proposals are more detailed than others. For example, on the Special Products, the proposal of the G20 says: "Having regard to their rural development and food security needs, developing countries shall benefit from … the establishment of Special Products … under conditions to be determined in the negotiations." And on the SSM, the G20 says: "Under conditions to be determined in the negotiations, a special safeguard mechanism (SSM) shall be established for use by developing countries, the scope of which would depend on the impact of tariff cuts ..." (WT/MIN(03)/W/6 of 4 September 2003).

On SP and SSM, the G33 says: "The G33 believes that the issue of SP and SSM is crucial in addressing food and livelihood security as well as rural development, and hence … there must be a stand-alone category for SP, … there must be no tariff reduction commitment for all SP… developing countries must be able to decide themselves which products they consider as SP ... SSM shall be established for use by developing countries … products considered as SP must also have access to SSM" (JOB(04)/65 of 1 June 2004).

An earlier proposal of the Africa Group goes into more detail and suggests specific elements for the criteria, types of measures and procedures for the special safeguard to be used by the developing countries (JOB(02)/187 of 20 November 2002).

These proposals appear very similar in approach and substance on SP and SSM, though some of them give more details at this stage while the others leave the details for the negotiations. The G20 proposal that the scope of the SSM would depend on the impact of tariff cuts may give an impression of being somewhat restrictive, but does not go against the G33 proposal in substance. The selection of SP and the treatment to be given to them and the application of the SSM will be decided in the negotiations and there is enough opportunity for further aligning these individual proposals.

On addressing the effects of the erosion of preferences, some proposals are brief while others are more detailed. For example, the G20 proposal says that "the question of preference erosion shall be addressed (in the negotiations)", while the Africa Group proposal goes into specifics and suggests that there should be minimum economic cost of erosion and a holistic approach in addressing it in coordination with other international organizations. It also suggests that the implementation of the market-access commitments of African countries should be postponed until the developed countries have eliminated their domestic support and export subsidies. Though there is a difference in the level of details, the substance is not different.

Having thus covered the negotiating framework and the proposals of the developing countries, we now proceed to discuss what their approach and follow-up action should be.

## SUGGESTIONS: WHAT SHOULD BE DONE?

### *CURRENT INEQUITIES*

It is well known by now that the current WTO agreements, which emerged out of the Uruguay Round of negotiations, are full of inequities and imbalances and mostly act against the developmental interests of the developing countries. The AoA is particularly so.[10] It is grossly weighted in favour of the developed countries and against the interests of the developing countries.

Some examples will make this abundantly clear. The developed countries were required under the AoA to reduce some of their domestic subsidies (those categorized under the Amber Box) by 20 percent and their budgetary outlay for export subsidies by 36 percent over six years (1995-2000). Thus they could retain these subsidies at levels as high as 80 percent and 64 percent respectively. Further, a significant part of their domestic subsidies, the ones covered by the Blue Box and Green Box, was totally exempt from any reduction. They also fixed very high tariffs as equivalent to their non-tariff measures and were required to reduce them by only 36 percent over the same six-year period. In addition, they could use the Special Safeguard measure (SSG) to protect their farmers. Besides, the "peace clause" in Article 13 of the AoA made their subsidies immune from any counteraction, whereby no countervailing duty could be imposed even if these subsidies caused injury to domestic production elsewhere.

Subsequent measures and policies of the major developed countries exacerbated the already grossly unfair situation. The US and the EU reduced their Amber Box subsidies as required, but enhanced their non-reducible subsidies (Blue Box and Green Box), thus actually increasing their total domestic subsidies rather than reducing them.

Theoretically, the developing countries could also make use of the AoA provisions on domestic subsidies, but, in practice, they could not, as they did not have the financial resources. There are very few developing countries that provide subsidies to agriculture, and that too at low levels only. In addition, the criteria for invoking the SSG were fixed in such a manner that the developing countries, with few exceptions, could not use it.

The developing countries were thus faced with a gravely iniquitous situation in having to compete with the highly subsidized production and exports of the developed countries while being unable to resort to the SSG to protect their farmers.

The AoA also had a serious structural deficiency in that those distorting agricultural trade were actually accorded higher advantages and flexibility. For example, those countries which had high Amber Box subsidies in the beginning could retain them at a substantially high level, while those not having them earlier could not subsequently use them beyond the *de minimis* level. Worse was the situation with regard to export subsidies. Those having high levels in the beginning could retain these subsidies at substantially high levels, while those which had not used them in the beginning could not apply them ever. And there was a similar ironical situation in respect of the SSG. The criterion for its application was such that those distorting the trade through non-tariff measures before the AoA came into force were allowed to use the SSG, while those which had not distorted the trade in this manner were not allowed this facility of protection.

As mentioned earlier, with the advent of the new negotiations in the Doha Work Programme, an opportunity has now come to remove, or at least reduce significantly, the inequities, imbalances and deficiencies in this area.

## *OBJECTIVES OF DEVELOPING COUNTRIES*

In light of what has been discussed above, it is abundantly clear that the current multilateral framework in agriculture is a carve-out for the major developed countries to protect their domestic production and ensure expanded exports. It is heavily weighted against the developing countries even though this sector is of vital importance in their national economies as a large section of their population depends on agriculture for sustenance. Besides, agriculture is taken up in most of the developing countries not as a commercial operation for profit, but as a means of sustenance in the absence of alternative professions. Fitting their agricultural economy into the market-price complex of the GATT/WTO system is already improper in the first place. On top of it, their weak agriculture economy faces grossly unfair competition from the highly subsidized agriculture of the major developed countries.

With all this in view, the objectives of the developing countries in the limited context of the current negotiations will naturally be to: (i) protect their domestic production against the onslaught of subsidized imports from the major developed countries; and (ii) expand the opportunity to export their own agricultural products.

In light of these objectives and the need to remove the current inequities and unfairness in this sector, the most rational approach will be to ask for the total abolition of domestic subsidies and export subsidies of all kinds in the developed countries before the developing countries themselves are called upon to undertake further obligations of tariff reduction. Reducing their tariffs while the domestic subsidies and export subsidies still continue in the developed countries will aggravate the inequity in the system and expose the agriculture of the developing countries to serious danger.

Though the negotiations are split, for convenience, into the three separate areas of market access, domestic support and export subsidies, the necessary sequential link between total removal of domestic subsidies and export subsidies in the developed countries on the one hand and further reduction of tariffs in the developing countries on the other should always be kept in view.

With this basic approach in mind, let us now turn to the three separate areas.

### *EXPORT SUBSIDIES*

If high tariffs in agriculture in the developed countries are an impropriety and domestic subsidies of all kinds are unfair, export subsidies, even in small amounts, are downright sinful. One may appreciate to some extent the relevance of measures taken in support of weak farmers, but to push exports with the aid of export subsidies and thus destroy the means of livelihood of the poor farmers of the developing countries cannot be considered rational at all. Clearly it must stop.

Helpfully, the July 04 decision provides for a date to be set for the elimination of export subsidies and equivalent measures with repayment periods beyond 180 days. The task now is to fix this end date and work out the modalities for proceeding to that end date.

There are three elements in the framework that guide the fixing of the end date: (i) it should be "credible" (para 17); (ii) the process of elimination will be implemented by "annual instalments" (para 20); and (iii) it will "take into account the need for some coherence" with internal reform steps of Members (para 20).

Point (i) suggests a short time frame for elimination, while point (ii) suggests a time frame of more than one year. Point (iii) refers primarily to the EU's internal reform process, mentioned earlier, that envisages continuing export subsidies for a long time. The formulation in point (iii), however, does not entail any compulsion, and rightly so. The elimination of this unfair practice cannot be guided by the subjectively fixed calendar of an individual Member, as the Member will naturally be most disinclined to be hurried in eliminating its measures. In conformity with points (i) and (ii), therefore, it may be appropriate for the developing countries to ask for elimination of these measures in two years at most, with a high degree of reduction, say up to at least 90 percent, in the first year.

In the background given above, the developing countries may further elaborate on their proposals regarding the export subsidies of the developed countries. Some suggestions are given below.

(i) The developed countries should eliminate export subsidies and equivalent measures with repayment periods beyond 180 days in two years, with reduction of up to at least 90 percent in the first year.

(ii) The disciplines in respect of equivalent measures with repayment periods of up to 180 days should be such that the subsidy components are removed. To that end, the interest rates, payment of interest and premium requirements should be fully aligned with the prevalent commercial rates/practices.

(iii) Disciplines on food aid may be sought by limiting it to actual aid. The country where it is given and the time when it is given should be determined by examining whether there is a "need" for food and absence of purchasing capacity. Paragraph 18 mentions the role of international organizations. This role may be in the form of certification of "need" and "absence of purchasing capacity". The international organization may also act as a trustee, receiving and distributing the food stock provided by a country as aid. Or the aid may simply be provided in the form of cash by the donor countries. All these precautions will take care of the interests of the LDCs and NFIDCs, which are a matter of concern in some of the proposals of the developing countries. When there is a need for food combined with absence of purchasing capacity in these countries, food aid should not be hampered.

(iv) For the developing countries, the provisions of Articles 9.4 and 12 of the AoA should continue.

## *DOMESTIC SUPPORT*

The developing countries have lost this round of battle to eliminate the Amber Box, Blue Box and Green Box subsidies of the developed countries. The framework merely provides for "substantial reduction" of the Amber Box subsidies, a ceiling on Blue Box subsidies, and review and clarification of Green Box subsidies to ensure that they have "no, or at most minimal, trade-distorting effects or effects on production". However, the range of options in each of these areas is large, as mentioned earlier. Naturally, in the context of the developing countries' objectives of protecting their domestic production and removing/reducing unfair competition in the export market, the permissible options should be used to their maximum advantage. Accordingly, it will be rational to choose the options that can reduce the domestic subsidies of the developed countries, irrespective of the "colour", to the maximum extent.

Taking first the Blue Box subsidies, paragraph 15 says that these "will not exceed 5%" of a Member's agricultural production. Thus it fixes a ceiling, not a norm. But given the way this issue has been covered in various other provisions of Annex A, there may be an expectation that a country is entitled to use Blue Box subsidies up to the extent of 5 percent. In fact, paragraph 15 itself mentions some possible upper shift from this ceiling limit in cases where a Member has high levels of Blue Box subsidies at present (a clear reference to the EU). In spite of all these stipulations, however, the fact remains that 5 percent is given as a ceiling, thus lower levels are permissible. As such, if the developing countries ask for lower levels of Blue Box subsidies in the developed countries, they will not be violating Annex A provisions.

Then, paragraph 13 gives criteria for two alternative types of Blue Box subsidies: one that is given under production-limiting programmes (used at present by the EU) and the other that does not require production (to cover the use by the US). But there is an overriding provision in paragraph 14 that the criteria "along with additional criteria will be negotiated". As the criteria are still to be "negotiated", neither of these alternative types can be considered to be agreed. Both of them are very much open at present. Hence the developing countries will be fully within their rights to disagree with the criteria, thus making the Blue Box subsidies inoperational.

In any case, it will be fully rational for them not to agree to the second set of criteria that allows for new users of Blue Box subsidies. Inequity and distortion of trade and production have already been brought about by use of the current Blue Box subsidies by the EU. Expansion of the criteria, thus enabling the US to also use the Blue Box, will further enhance the inequity and distortion. It will be a retrograde step on the way to reforming agricultural trade and thus militate against the objectives of the Doha Declaration. If the US and the EU want to have parity and parallelism between their practices, it must not be at the cost of the developing countries' farmers.

With regard to overall reduction, the total of the Amber Box, Blue Box and *de minimis* subsidies in the first year of implementation "will not exceed 80 percent" of a base level (para 7). It is given as the ceiling and not the norm, as discussed earlier. Hence it is very much permissible to ask for a lower level in the first year than 80 percent of the base level.

The Green Box subsidies are to be disciplined by reviewing and clarifying the criteria. There is a grave need and large scope in this area, as the current rules are very general and leave great possibility for subjective action. The provisions are also very open-ended in terms of the size of subsidy. It is through this loophole that the major developed countries have succeeded in reducing their reducible subsidies and yet enhancing the total subsidies by increasing the subsidies under various provisions of the Green Box.

The pretence about the Green Box subsidies is that they do not distort trade. This is very much a false pretence, as these payments, which are not in the nature of any general welfare assistance but are given only to farmers, enhance the farmers' economic capacity to continue with their unviable agricultural production. To that extent, the Green Box subsidies do encourage and support uneconomic production, thus distorting production and trade. Furthermore, the eligibility criteria are very loose and there is no upper limit. For example, paragraph 6 in Annex 2 of the AoA on "decoupled income support" allows payment to the farmers without any ceiling and with quite open eligibility criteria. Paragraph 10 in Annex 2 of the AoA, which is about subsidies for resource retirement programmes, imposes a limitation that the land will not be used for marketable agricultural production for at least three years; but this means that the farmer can thus revert to production on the land in three years' time. Then paragraph 11 of Annex 2 includes investment aid for overcoming structural disadvantages. There is little logic in treating all this as non-trade-distorting.

Annex A now asks for a review and clarification of Green Box criteria with the objective of ensuring that Green Box subsidies have "no, or at most minimal, trade-distorting effects or effects on production". Herein lies an opportunity for the developing countries to set the criteria in such a way that the elements in the Green Box that are patently trade-distorting or production-distorting are taken out of this list.

In this background, the proposals and thrust of the developing countries in respect of the domestic subsidies of the developed countries may be as follows:

(i) In paragraph 13, the second alternative set of criteria that expands the scope of the Blue Box by opening the possibility for new entrants to the Blue Box should be rejected.

(ii) Existing Blue Box subsidies should be substantially reduced in the first year of implementation (the 5-percent stipulation in paragraph 15 is, after all, the upper limit and not a norm) and then be progressively reduced substantially, say at least 80 percent, during the implementation period.
(iii) The *de minimis* provision for the developed countries should be removed.
(iv) The overall reduction of trade-distorting support (para 7) should be substantial in the first year and the total support should be much lower than 80 percent of the base level.
(v) In the AMS (para 9), the objective of substantial reduction should be achieved by eliminating the bulk of it, say 80 percent, in the implementation period.
(vi) In relation to the Green Box subsidies (para 16), the so-called decoupled support and investment subsidies in Annex 2 of the AoA should be removed right in the beginning of the implementation period. The former is a type of payment that artificially enhances the staying capacity of a farmer and is thus clearly production-distorting and trade-distorting. The latter is a form of direct payment to support investment and may also play a role in artificially enhancing the staying capacity of a farmer in agriculture, thus distorting production and trade.
(vii) Some other Green Box payments, like those for insurance, natural disasters, environment and regional development, should have objective criteria for eligibility and have limits imposed on their amount and duration.
(viii) For the developing countries, the *de minimis* subsidies should be continued. Further, exemption from reduction for subsidies in Article 6.2 of the AoA should continue, with the clarification that the input subsidy is not only for low-income and resource-poor farmers. After all, farmers in general, perhaps with very few exceptions, in the developing countries have serious handicaps in production and trade.

## *MARKET ACCESS*

There are three basic stipulations in Annex A for the mechanism of tariff reduction: (i) there will be a single approach for developed- and developing-country Members to meet the objectives of the Doha mandate (para 28); (ii) the formula of reduction should take into account the different tariff structures of developed and developing countries (para 28); and (iii) the number of bands, the criteria for defining them and the type of tariff reduction in them are all to be negotiated (para 30). Thus what has been determined is that there will be bands, but their formation and the treatment within them are all yet to be decided.

With this current flexibility, in the light of the range of options available under Annex A and the approach and interests of the developing countries as discussed earlier, the proposals and the thrust from the side of the developing countries may be as follows:

(i) Working on paragraphs 28 and 30, there should be separate sets of bands for the developed countries and the developing countries. Also, there should be separate ways of tariff reduction in these two respective sets of bands. (The stipulation of “a single approach … (that) meets all the objectives of the Doha mandate” does not appear to prohibit it. The approach could be “single” in the sense of having substantial reduction in tariffs and greater reduction in higher tariffs, but considering that the different tariff structures of developed and developing countries have to be taken into account and the criteria of formation of bands and treatment within the bands are still open, nothing prohibits having separate sets of bands and separate formulas for the developing and developed countries.)

(ii) In the bands of the developed countries, the Swiss formula should be applied, with different coefficients in different bands, ensuring deeper cuts in bands with higher tariffs. (As will be explained in the chapter on NAMA, the lower the coefficient in the Swiss formula, the deeper is the resulting cut.)

(iii) The sensitive products of the developed countries should be limited in number. They should be placed in the respective bands and given comparatively softer (i.e., higher) coefficients within these bands. Keeping them out of these bands altogether will not be consistent with paragraph 31 that prohibits “undermining the overall objective of the tiered approach”. The availability of softer coefficients should be accompanied by tariff quota provisions and expansion of tariff quota.

(iv) Tariff escalation in the developed countries should be tackled (para 36) by having a multiplier for tariff reduction for the processed product as compared to that for the primary product. Alternatively, irrespective of the bands, in the product chain, the tariff should be made equal on the primary product, intermediate processed product and final processed product.

(v) Tariff peaks in the developed countries should be tackled (para 30) by having a ceiling on the tariffs.

(vi) The Special Safeguard for the developed countries should be discontinued. They may resort to only the general safeguard provisions when necessary.

(vii) For the developing countries, there may be simply one band and the formula of reduction should be based on average reduction of tariffs with the stipulation of a certain minimum reduction in each tariff line. The number of Special

Products may be stipulated as a percentage of the total number of agricultural products, but the selection of SP should be made by the developing country concerned. These products should not be covered by the tariff-reduction formula. There should be a Special Safeguard Mechanism for the developing countries that is effective and conveniently useable and available for all products.

(Some developing countries are concerned with expanding market access for their exports in other developing countries. Instead of the WTO agriculture negotiations, however, they should use a different route to achieve this objective, i.e., the route of the Global System of Trade Preferences (GSTP). Under the GSTP, which is serviced by the United Nations Conference on Trade and Development (UNCTAD), the tariff reduction will apply only to developing countries' products and not those of the developed countries. The special advantage of taking the GSTP route towards this end is further elaborated in the chapter on NAMA.)

(viii) Preference erosion should be effectively addressed and the cooperation of other international organizations in this regard should also be sought.

(ix) Non-tariff barriers must be addressed in the negotiations and solutions regarding them worked out. Addressing NTBs effectively should be an integral part of the exercise in view of the objective of "substantial improvements in market access" as called for in the Doha Declaration and recalled in Annex A. Generally there is a tendency to leave NTBs as a residual item at the end of meetings/negotiations, with the result that it does not get proper attention. However, it is as important as tariffs, hence the negotiations on tariffs and NTBs should proceed in parallel. Some NTBs may be handled in the negotiating group on agriculture. Some others may be handled by other WTO bodies, but there is a need to give them priority and link progress on this front to the work on market access in the negotiating group on agriculture. One method may be to negotiate these items in special sessions of these respective WTO bodies. Progress reports should then be made available to each session of the negotiating group on agriculture, so that parallel progress on tariffs and NTBs is ensured.

### *OVERALL*

There are certain other important elements that cut across the three areas into which the agriculture negotiations are divided. These are explained below.

(i) It is important to have a proper sequence of decisions while moving towards the conclusion of the negotiations. The developing countries should first settle (even provisionally) the criteria, related percentages and ceilings in the area of domestic subsidies before settling the criteria and percentages on tariffs. Further, the settlement of criteria and percentages on tariffs should go hand in hand with progress on NTBs.

(ii) It is important to work out the elements of the SSM on a priority basis. This should be brought right to the top of the priority list. Only after knowing what type of defensive mechanism is available to them should the developing countries work on the type of tariff concessions they are prepared to make. Further, the shape of the SSM will also give them an idea of their defence against the domestic subsidies and export subsidies of the developed countries. Hence, the SSM should not be considered merely as an issue to be addressed in the market-access pillar. It is also vitally linked with the defence against the subsidized imports from the major developed countries.

(iii) Now it appears that the developing countries may not be able to have all the subsidies of the developed countries eliminated quickly. Perhaps the developed countries have their own compulsions in retaining some of these subsidies. But it should not be at the cost of the developing countries, whose farming sector will remain exposed to the extended risk of unfair competition. Some way must be found to correct this situation. One option may be to suspend the implementation of the tariff commitments of the developing countries until the developed countries have eliminated their subsidies.

# Chapter 3

# NON-AGRICULTURAL MARKET ACCESS (NAMA)

## FRAMEWORK

THE framework for the negotiations on non-agricultural market access is contained in the Doha Declaration and Annex B to the July 04 decision (henceforth simply called Annex B). Serious controversy surrounded the passage of this annex, however, with the result that it has become almost inoperative. A little background is necessary to understand the status of Annex B.

The chairman of the negotiating group on NAMA had presented the text of what he thought would be the consensus in the group. A large number of developing countries, however, disagreed with the text and his approach. It is reported that he nevertheless still insisted on sending this text to the General Council. On continued and persistent protests from a large number of the developing countries, a suggestion was made that a "vehicle" would accompany the text. This "vehicle" was to be in the nature of some form of reservation and was proposed to be placed somewhere in the General Council decision, totally separate from Annex B. But Annex B was proposed to be "adopted" by the General Council, thus rendering the "vehicle" very much meaningless. This was naturally not acceptable to a very large number of the developing countries. They are reported to have insisted on making the paragraph of reservation an integral part of Annex B itself. As a result, the current paragraph 1 was placed in Annex B and became an integral part of it.

The other paragraphs of Annex B contain elements on important aspects of NAMA in the nature of a framework for commitments in the NAMA negotiations. But paragraph 1 of Annex B (henceforward paragraph numbers in this chapter will refer to paragraphs in Annex B, unless otherwise stated) nullifies all that. It says that Annex B contains "the initial elements" for future work and adds that "additional negotiations are required to reach agreement on the specifics of some of these elements". These elements are then enumerated and they cover almost all the important parts of Annex B. To be specific, the elements mentioned for additional negotiations are: formula (which is covered in paras 4 and 5), unbound tariffs in indent 2 of paragraph 5 (already included in formula), flexibilities for developing countries and the issue of a sectoral tariff component (paras 6-13), and preferences (para 16). Thus what is left of Annex B besides paragraph 1 and the elements to be negotiated further is paragraph 2 reaffirming the Doha objective, paragraph 3 acknowledging the previous work, paragraph 14 relating to NTBs and paragraph 15 on studies and capacity-building.

Given this status of Annex B, it cannot be taken to be the framework of the negotiations at this stage. It is at best relevant only as an indicator of the wishlist of the major developed countries, since it amply accommodates their interests. In view of what happened in the July 2004 negotiations, however, it is likely that there will still be pressure on the developing countries to continue the negotiations on the basis of Annex B. Efforts may be made to persuade them to start negotiating specific percentages and numbers here and there in Annex B, while keeping its frame intact. But they will be fully within their rights to reject this approach, as the essential elements of Annex B do not have the status of having been accepted; they are still to be negotiated. With Annex B in such a position, the only framework for further negotiations is the Doha Declaration.

Paragraph 16 of the Doha Declaration, which is on NAMA, has the following four elements:

(i) There should be reduction/elimination of tariffs, including tariff peaks, high tariffs and tariff escalation, as also non-tariff barriers, in particular on the products of export interest to the developing countries.
(ii) The product coverage should be comprehensive, without any *a priori* exclusions.
(iii) The special needs and interests of the developing countries and LDCs will be taken fully into account.
(iv) There will be less than full reciprocity by the developing countries and LDCs in the reduction of tariffs.

This constitutes the current framework of the negotiations. A detailed framework will involve working out the modalities for the manner in which tariffs will be reduced/eliminated, incorporating in that process special treatment to the developing countries, including the LDCs. This is what the exercise on Annex B attempted to do but failed. Now it has to be done afresh.

## RANGE OF OPTIONS[11]

For the reduction/elimination of tariffs, the first step is to work out the formula that will be followed and then the treatment within the formula. Also, approaches for other elements of the framework, like tariff peaks, NTBs, etc., will have to be worked out. The options, and sometimes the extreme ends of the range of options, are given below. Naturally, the final choices will lie somewhere between these extremes:

(i) The same or similar formula for tariff reduction may be applicable to both the developed countries and the developing countries.

Or

There may be separate formulas for the developed countries and developing countries.

(ii) The formula may be linear, i.e., requiring a simple percentage cut on the current bound tariffs.

Or

It may be non-linear, where higher tariffs are subjected to comparatively deeper cuts. One common form of non-linear formula is the so-called Swiss formula.

(iii) In the non-linear formula of the Swiss formula type, the depth of tariff cut depends on the value of the coefficient used in the formula, as will be explained later. Thus the coefficient may be such that the cuts are very deep.

Or

The coefficient may be such that there is a comparatively smaller cut.

(iv) For tariff peaks and high tariffs, there may be several options. There may be a ceiling on the tariffs.

Or

There may be a limitation that no tariff will be above a certain multiple of the average tariff for the country.

Or

There may be a simple application of a non-linear formula with an appropriate coefficient that results in substantial cuts.

(v) For tariff escalation, again there may be some options. The tariff on a product in processed form may not exceed that on the product in primary form.

Or

The tariff reduction for a product in processed form may be much higher than that for the product in primary form.

(vi) For non-tariff barriers, there may be different methods of handling reduction/ elimination. These may all be addressed in the NAMA negotiating group and a certain degree of parallelism may be observed between progress on NTBs and on tariffs.

Or

The issue of NTBs may be handled separately in various specialized WTO bodies, with an appropriate mechanism to monitor the progress in the NAMA negotiating group.

(vii) For the sectoral approach to tariff elimination, there may be different options. The approach may simply be abandoned. (For an explanation of this approach, see the section on "Sectoral liberalization" in this chapter.)

Or

Certain sectors may be selected for zero tariff/special reduction commitment. Normally the selection of the sectors will involve finding an appropriate balance in respect of some elements, e.g., export interests and import potential of the countries participating in this exercise.

(viii) Participation in the zero-tariff exercise may be compulsory for all Members (excluding the LDCs).

Or

The developing countries may have the option of either joining in the zero-tariff exercise or remaining out of it. Of course, through the operation of the most-favoured-nation (MFN) principle in the WTO, they will in any case get the benefit of zero tariff of others.

Or

Out of the products selected for zero tariff or very low tariff, the developing countries may have the option of choosing a minimum specified number of products.

All these are totally open questions at the current stage of the negotiations and thus the developing countries have the opportunity to select the options that are best suited to them and pursue them in the negotiations. It is very likely that the major developed countries will advance the argument that the specific elements have already been included in Annex B and all that is needed now is to fill in the percentages at various places. But this is totally incorrect as paragraph 1 of Annex B has kept all this open. Thus nothing, other than what is in the Doha Declaration, should be considered as settled or agreed. Considering the recent trend of work in the NAMA negotiating group, however, it is anticipated that the developing countries will be put under severe pressure; hence they have to be very resolute in their stand.

In this background and in the context of these ranges of options, let us now consider the proposals that have been submitted by the developing countries in the current negotiations.

## PROPOSALS OF DEVELOPING COUNTRIES

The developing countries, individually or in groups, have submitted a large number of proposals, and many of them are quite specific. Their proposals, along with those of the developed countries, have been summarized and put together by the WTO Secretariat in document TN/MA/6/Rev.1 of 1 April 2003. A chart in tabular form at the end of that paper delineates the positions of various Members in different areas.

It may be relevant to enumerate some of the detailed and specific papers of the developing countries. This will give an idea of the broad interest that the developing countries have in this subject. Some of these papers are: TN/MA/W/27 of 18 February 2003 from Ghana, Kenya, Nigeria, Tanzania, Uganda, Zambia and Zimbabwe; TN/MA/W/31 of 25 March 2003 from Egypt, India, Indonesia, Kenya, Malaysia, Mauritius, Nigeria, Tanzania, Uganda and Zimbabwe; TN/MA/W/40 of 11 August 2003 from Ghana, Kenya, Madagascar, Mauritius, Nigeria, Rwanda, Tanzania, Tunisia, Uganda, Zambia and Zimbabwe; TN/MA/W/10 of 22 October 2002, Add. 1 of 8 January 2003, Add. 2 of 18 March 2003 and Add. 3 of 10 April 2003 from India; TN/MA/W/23 of 15 January 2003 from Brazil; TN/MA/W/45 of 1 September 2003 from Argentina, Bolivia, Brazil, Chile, Colombia, Costa Rica, Ecuador, El Salvador, Guatemala, Mexico, Panama, Paraguay, Peru, Uruguay and Venezuela; TN/MA/W/30 of 25 March 2003 from Barbados, Jamaica and Trinidad and Tobago; TN/MA/W/47 of 30 March 2004 from the ACP countries; and TN/MA/W/38 of 16 June 2003 from Fiji.

These proposals generally ask for fast reduction of tariffs in the developed countries, in particular of tariff peaks, high tariffs and tariff escalation. There is a preference for a simple and user-friendly formula. A linear percentage reduction has been favoured, with higher percentage reduction for the developed countries than for the developing countries. Tariff peaks in the developed countries are sought to be reduced by stipulating that no tariff will be higher than three times the average tariff of a developed country. Reduction/elimination of tariff escalation is sought to be effectively addressed.

On the sectoral approach, it has been proposed that zero-for-zero tariff should be optional for the developing countries.

In respect of the developing countries, flexibility is proposed for keeping some tariff lines unbound and binding some of the current unbound tariffs at above the highest levels for the bound items. Further, the implementation period is sought to be longer compared to that for the developed countries.

It is proposed that the LDCs should not have an obligation to reduce their tariffs. The developed countries should also allow duty-free access to the products of LDCs.

It has been suggested that an effective mechanism and measures should be established to address the adverse effects of erosion of preferences.

Addressing NTBs effectively has also been considered important.

## SUGGESTIONS: WHAT SHOULD BE DONE?

### *PAST EXPERIENCE AND CURRENT SITUATION*

There is a significant difference in tariff structure between the developed countries and the developing countries. In the developed countries, the average tariff is relatively low, but tariffs on the products of export interest to the developing countries are relatively very high. As the developed countries do not really need the revenue from tariffs, the main objective of these high tariffs appears to be to protect their domestic industry. This differential emerged out of historical reasons relating to the negotiations. The developed countries have reduced their tariffs generally in consideration of their mutual interest. As the developing countries had not been much engaged in this exercise prior to the Uruguay Round, they could not influence the tariff-reduction process in the developed countries, with the result that the tariffs in those countries remained comparatively very high on the products of export interest to the developing countries. This was in spite of existing provisions on special and differential treatment of the developing countries, which were not seriously implemented by the developed countries in respect of their tariffs. It is important to note this historical evolution of tariffs in the developed countries, particularly as it has a direct bearing on calls from the developed countries for reduction of tariffs in the developing countries, as will be explained later.

The tariffs in the developing countries, particularly the bound levels, are comparatively high. Some developing countries have had to reduce their tariffs to low levels to fulfil the conditions for obtaining structural adjustment loans from international financial institutions. But many of them have not bound them in the GATT/WTO.

Tariffs are important instruments for the developing countries, both for revenue generation and for protection of their domestic industry. With practically no scope now for imposing any quantitative restrictions on imports, the only instrument of protection available to them is the tariff. Herein lies the importance of tariffs in their development process. Experience has shown that measured and modulated protection of the domestic industry on a dynamic basis has helped industrialization and upgradation of technology.

For example, at a country's lower stage of development, a machine may have to be imported liberally to produce some consumer items. It may be desirable to keep the tariff on this machine low at that stage to encourage imports of this machine so that the production of the consumer items is facilitated. At a later stage of development, however, the country may decide to manufacture this machine itself. It may then be necessary to raise the tariff on the machine so that its domestic production is facilitated by protection against imports. At a still later stage of development, the industry producing this machine in the country may have become fully mature and may not need protection against imports anymore. At that stage, the country may again decide to lower the tariff on this machine, as the domestic firms producing the machine are already fully competitive in the international market. In this manner, there is a desirable sequence of "low tariff - high tariff - low tariff" phases for various industrial products. If a country were to bind its tariffs at low levels at the initial stage of development, however, it may not be able to develop its industrial production later and its options will be foreclosed right in the beginning.

The difference between voluntarily having a low tariff on a product and binding the tariff at a low level in the WTO should be clearly understood. The former can be a part of the dynamic process of development that may require a low tariff on a product at a particular stage, with the option of raising the tariff later if need be. The latter, however, removes the possibility of raising the tariff beyond the bound level, thus constraining development options in the future. If a country finds it convenient to keep the tariff on a product low for domestic reasons, it may do so without undertaking an obligation in the WTO to bind it at the low level.

Recent experience has also shown that hurried trade liberalization has resulted in deindustrialization in many developing countries. There are several instances of this malady in Africa and the Caribbean region.

In this background, one should try to understand why a very large number of the developing countries are cautious about their tariff reduction. And they are generally reluctant to undertake a binding commitment for tariff reduction in the GATT/WTO, as such a commitment will prevent them from retracing their steps should the need arise. Many of them are still engaged in experiments on their development and in that phase it is important for them to keep their options open so that there may be a possibility for making corrections in mid-course. But this is precisely what will be precluded by their binding of tariffs in the GATT/WTO.

For all these reasons, the Doha Declaration has made a specific stipulation about the special needs and interests of the developing countries. The developed countries should therefore take it seriously rather than consider it as an obstacle in their efforts to prise open the markets of the developing countries.

## *ASPECTS OF RIGHTS AND OBLIGATIONS*

Then there is also the important aspect of rights and obligations involved in the exercise of tariff reduction. Countries' bound tariff levels have generally evolved through the process of tariff negotiations over various rounds of multilateral trade negotiations as a result of exchange of concessions among countries. The current bound and unbound tariff levels, including those in the developing countries, are the existing rights of the countries. The developing countries do not have to be on the defensive in retaining high tariffs; it is their current right in the GATT/WTO system. As a counterpart of it, the developed countries have continued to impose high tariffs on the products of interest to the developing countries while they have significantly reduced the tariffs on the products of mutual interest among themselves.

It has been argued that the developing countries have gained in the past through the route of MFN treatment without making much tariff concessions themselves. It is true that the developing countries did get the benefit of the tariff reductions, but again this was their right through the operation of the MFN treatment which, being in Article I of the General Agreement on Tariffs and Trade (GATT) 1994, confers this right to all the contracting parties to the GATT. It is a part of the rights and obligations in the system. Moreover, it has to be noted that the developed countries also benefited from the developing countries' taking advantage of the tariff reductions, because, through the development of the developing countries in this manner, the developed countries enjoyed expanded markets for their own exports and other expanded opportunities in these countries. Thus extension of tariff benefits to the developing countries by the operation of the MFN clause has brought benefits to both developing and developed countries.

A more basic issue involved here is that the tariff negotiations are not about compensation for past gains or losses; they are future-oriented and are based on future gains and opportunities. Thus the developing countries will naturally base their approach in these negotiations on their perception of the gains or losses emerging from these negotiations in future.

Thus any commitment on tariff reduction that the developing countries make in the current negotiations should be with the aim of getting at least commensurate benefits from the "more than reciprocal" tariff concessions from the developed countries.

It is also argued sometimes that the developing countries should lower their tariffs in order to improve the market access of the goods of other developing countries. This is true, but the NAMA tariff negotiations in the WTO are not an appropriate forum for this purpose. A more appropriate route to achieve this objective is through mutual tariff concessions among the developing countries in the framework of the Global System of Trade Preferences that is serviced by UNCTAD. The special benefit of the GSTP route is that the tariff concessions made by the developing countries within this framework are only extended to other developing countries and not to the developed countries. This has several advantages for the developing countries as compared to reduction of tariffs in the NAMA exercise.

Firstly, since the benefit is extended only to the developing countries, their exporters get special advantage over those of the developed countries who do not receive this benefit. The exporters of the developing countries will face less competition to that extent. Secondly, the producers in the importing developing countries are less exposed to the risk of competition from imports, as the imports from the developed countries will not get this benefit. Thirdly, the importing developing countries will face less tariff loss for the same reason. Fourthly, there may be an incidental, but important, benefit in as much as it may encourage investment in the developing countries, since the production in these countries will have enhanced market access in other developing countries.

This does not, however, mean that the developing countries should not enter into tariff negotiations in the NAMA exercise in the WTO. They should certainly participate in it fully, but their objective and strategy here should be to make tariff concessions only with the aim of getting adequate and appropriate concessions from the developed countries in return.

## *OBJECTIVES OF DEVELOPING COUNTRIES*

The main objectives of the developing countries in the NAMA negotiations should naturally be: (i) to expand their export opportunities primarily in the developed countries; and (ii) to protect their domestic production as may be necessary and desirable in their development process. (As explained above, the objective of expanding export opportunities in other developing countries should be primarily achieved through serious engagement in the GSTP exercise, where a new round of negotiations was recently launched.)

They should sponsor and support the mechanism/formula for tariff reduction that can fulfil these objectives.

## *TARIFF REDUCTION*

### *Formula*

The agreed method of tariff reduction in the current NAMA negotiations appears to be what is called the formula approach, i.e., tariff reduction in accordance with a formula or a set of formulas. An alternative method is the request-offer approach, but the current trends indicate that this is not going to be the norm in these negotiations. In the latter approach, two countries engage in making requests and offers regarding their mutual tariff reduction and each agrees to cut tariffs up to agreed levels on an agreed list of products. Naturally these products are those which are of export interest to the negotiating partner. Finally, the reduced levels of tariffs on these products are entered into the country's tariff schedules, and this benefit is thereby extended to all the other Members of the WTO through the operation of the MFN principle.

In comparison, in the formula approach, the extent of tariff cut depends on the type of formula used and various coefficients in the formula. A simple formula may be for cutting the average tariff, without specifying cuts in individual tariff lines. Alternatively, there may be a formula for cuts in individual tariff lines. This formula may be a simple linear formula, a simple non-linear formula or a complex non-linear formula. Some examples will be provided shortly.

It may be better for the developing countries not to adopt any formula that is applicable to individual tariff lines. They have not been required in any of the previous rounds of multilateral trade negotiations to adopt any line-by-line formula approach. Their obligation should at most be limited to reduction of their average tariff by a certain percentage without any stipulation about the individual tariff lines. The developing countries should have the flexibility to 'spread' the cut in the average tariff over their various tariff lines in accordance with their own developmental priorities. However, if at all they have to assume an obligation to apply a formula for individual tariff lines, it should be a simple linear formula which results in tariff cuts by a certain percentage. This is explained below.

For the developed countries, the developing countries should ask for use of a non-linear formula applicable to various tariff lines. But here too, they should not get involved with any complex non-linear formula which will be difficult to understand and where the results will be difficult to assess. In the current exercise, various types of formulas, including some complex ones, have been suggested. A complex formula makes it difficult to assess the additional export opportunities and additional risk of enhanced imports emerging from it. Besides, its implementation is also difficult. Hence the developing countries should prefer a simple non-linear formula even for the developed countries.

Examples of a simple linear formula and a simple non-linear formula are given below.

A simple linear formula is to cut the tariff by a certain percentage (percentage cut formula).

This is expressed as: $t_1 = c \times t_0$, where $t_0$ is the base tariff, c is the percentage factor and $t_1$ is the final tariff.

In this formula, a higher tariff is reduced by a greater absolute amount by virtue of a higher base for calculation of the reduction, but the *rate* of reduction is the same for all tariff levels. This formula was used as a basis among the developed countries in the Kennedy Round of multilateral trade negotiations (1964-68).

A slightly more complex formula is a non-linear formula, of which a simple variety is commonly called the Swiss formula.

This is expressed as: $t_1 = (a \times t_0)/(a + t_0)$, where $t_0$ is the base tariff, a is a coefficient and $t_1$ is the final tariff. A simple transformation makes it $1/t_1 - 1/t_0 = 1/a$, which means that the difference between the reciprocals of the final and initial tariffs is equal to the reciprocal of the coefficient.

In this formula, the rate of reduction for a higher tariff is greater than that for a lower one. This formula has a coefficient "a" that determines how big the reduction and the rate of reduction will be. A smaller "a" ensures a bigger reduction. For example, giving values of 5, 15 and 50 to "a", an initial tariff of 20 is reduced to final tariff levels of 4, 8.6 and 14.3 respectively. Then, for a given value 15 for "a", initial tariffs of 40 and 20 result respectively in the final tariffs of 10.9 and 8.6. This formula was used by some developed countries in the Tokyo Round of negotiations (1973-79).

The percentage cut formula is the simplest, as mentioned above. The non-linear Swiss formula is slightly more complex, yet not very difficult to operate on. But any formula that is more complex than these may become a burden on the developing country both in the negotiations and in actual implementation. For the linear formula, the negotiations will focus on the percentage of cut; while for the Swiss formula, the focus will be on the value of the coefficient.

The developing countries should seek to have separate formulas/methods for the developed countries' tariff reduction and for their own. The tariff structures of the developed countries and the developing countries are very different, hence a differential approach is rational. Further, the former should achieve greater reduction than the latter in consonance with the principles of "less than full reciprocity" and taking "fully into account the special needs and interests of the developing countries" as laid down in paragraph 16 of the Doha Declaration.

While choosing any formula, it is desirable that at least an approximate quantitative assessment is made of its possible results in terms of likely increases in exports and imports. A practical way for a developing country to do so may be to select about 20 products of export interest to it and make an assessment of the possible expansion of exports of these products if a particular formula is applied by the countries that are its main markets. Similarly it should select about 20 products that need protection from imports because of their sensitivity in the national economy and assess possible increases in imports if it uses a particular method or formula. These two assessments will help the developing country in making a balanced judgement about supporting or opposing a formula. The selection of the products for assessment and the assessment itself should be done on the basis of both the current situation and dynamic considerations, keeping in view the possible development path in the near future.

Some expertise is required to undertake these quantitative assessments. The developing countries may draw on the help of various institutions/organizations that are engaged in providing them with technical assistance. It may be even better to get the assessment done by two institutions/organizations and then decide on the method/formula, percentages, coefficients, etc.

### *Developed Countries' Tariff Reduction*

Let us first consider the choice of formula to be applicable for the developed countries. Their average tariffs are low, but there are tariff peaks and high tariffs on certain products which are of export interest to the developing countries and thus need to be focused on. A formula that merely reduces the average tariff will not be of advantage to the developing countries, as the reduction from the already low average level will not significantly improve their market access in the developed countries. Hence an "across-the-board formula" may not be very useful.

The target of the developing countries therefore should be deep cuts in the tariff peaks and high tariffs in the developed countries, and not merely reduction of average tariffs. They should prefer a formula that can achieve this target.

For an effective reduction in tariff peaks and high tariffs, some alternatives may be as follows:

(i) There may be a numerical ceiling on the developed countries' tariff levels.
(ii) Their highest tariff should be less than a particular multiple of their current average tariff.
(iii) They may follow the Swiss formula with a low value for "a".

The first two alternatives will result in a more direct lowering of the tariff peaks and high tariffs.

Here it is relevant to go back to Annex B, which, though not having the status of the basis of negotiations, is indicative of the approach of the major developed countries. Paragraph 4 of Annex B stipulates a non-linear formula for both developed and developing countries (with the exception of the LDCs). (We shall take up the case of the developing countries later.) This paragraph does not suggest any special means for reducing the tariff peaks and high tariffs of the developed countries. If the treatment of the tariff peaks and high tariffs of the developed countries is mixed up with the general tariff in the reduction formula, the developing countries will not get much benefit, as explained above.

However, if the third alternative is ultimately applied, as is the stipulation in paragraph 4, there should be separate treatment of the tariff peaks and high tariffs of the developed countries within the formula. Very low values of "a" in the Swiss formula should be applied for these tariffs.

There should be a simple method for identifying the tariff peaks and high tariffs. One method may be to define them as tariffs which are above a certain multiple of the current average level of industrial tariffs for the developed countries.

An example will clarify how a reduction in tariffs other than tariff peaks and high tariffs will not add significantly to market access in the developed countries. Their average tariff is about 4 percent at present. Thus if their average tariff or normal tariff is reduced even by 50 percent, it may only result in a reduction from, say, 4 percent to 2 percent. Thus if a US$100 product is imported in the developed country, the final prices before and after the tariff reduction will be US$104 and US$102 respectively. This will hardly result in any significant increase in market access. In comparison, let us see the effect of a deep cut in tariff peaks. The developed countries have tariff peaks and high tariffs even in the range of 25 to 30 percent. A formula which brings them down to about 10 percent will obviously result in an effective increase in market access. Hence there is a need to focus mainly on reducing tariff peaks and high tariffs in developed countries.

In short, it is in the interest of the developing countries to insist on formulas for tariff reduction in the developed countries that will result in deep cuts in their tariff peaks and high tariffs. Formulas that simply aim at reducing the average tariffs or reducing already low tariffs in the developed countries will not be of much use to the developing countries.

### *Developing Countries' Tariff Reduction and Binding*[12]

Developing countries have had flexibility in adopting the method of tariff reduction in past negotiations, including the Uruguay Round. They did not follow any particular formula; they, on the other hand, reduced their average tariffs. And while doing so, they had the flexibility of setting the levels of individual tariffs.

In consonance with paragraph 16 of the Doha Declaration, they should again have that flexibility.

Developing countries may also give concessions in yet another form, i.e., by binding some of their tariffs that are currently unbound. As they currently have the right to raise these tariffs to the levels of their choice, binding some of them will itself be a concession, as they commit thereby not to raise the tariff beyond the bound limit.

However, their concessions in the form of further binding of unbound tariffs and/or reducing their bound tariffs (through whatever method) should be contingent on substantial reduction of the tariff peaks and high tariffs of the developed countries and not merely on the developed countries' following a non-linear formula across the board. By just reducing to some extent their average tariffs or already low tariffs, the developed countries will not be giving any meaningful benefit to the developing countries in terms of expanded market access, when in fact they are expected to give much higher concessions than what is given by the developing countries in accordance with the "less than full reciprocity" principle.

Reciprocity should be measured in terms of enhanced market-access opportunities and not in terms of potential revenue loss, as was the consideration in the request-offer type of negotiations earlier.

We now return to Annex B to assess what the developed countries' expectation of the developing countries is with regard to tariff binding and tariff reduction. Paragraph 4 stipulates non-linear line-by-line tariff reduction for both developed and developing countries, with differentials for the developing countries. Further, the developing countries may have [10] percent of tariff lines (the square bracket indicates that the number is only indicative) subjected to less than formula cut (but not lower than half the formula cut) and [5] percent of tariff lines without binding or without formula cut. However, there is a limitation that the former should not cover more than [10] percent of the total value of the country's imports and the latter not more than [5] percent of the total value of imports (para 8). The developing countries having less than [35] percent of binding coverage will be exempted from formula cut but will be expected to have 100 percent binding coverage and a tariff average not higher than the overall average of the bound tariffs of all the developing countries (para 6).

These are very stringent requirements and the developing countries have rightly rejected them through paragraph 1. As has been explained earlier, however, since they were included in Annex B, it is very likely that the developed countries will try again to draw the developing countries into negotiations based on this format and discuss only the specific percentages. The trouble with such an approach is that the whole format itself is unsuitable for the developing countries and falls far short of the stipulation of taking account of the "special needs and interests" of the developing countries. Merely tinkering with the percentages while keeping the format intact will not be appropriate from the angle of the developing countries.

In summary, the developing countries should not accept the adoption of any non-linear formula, nor any formula that requires tariff reduction on a line-by-line basis. They should accept only a reduction of their average tariffs. The level of reduction of the average should be negotiated.

## *SECTORAL LIBERALIZATION*

There are proposals from the developed countries for a parallel route, viz., sectoral route of tariff reduction/elimination. In this process, tariffs in some selected sectors will be subjected to elimination (commonly called zero-for-zero method) or special reduction by all participants. Since tariffs are important for the developing countries in various ways as explained earlier, the sectoral approach, particularly the zero-for-zero method, should not be made compulsory for the developing countries. They should have the flexibility to either join in or opt out.

Whether the developing countries participate in this exercise should depend on: (i) whether zero tariff on a particular product included in this exercise gives them adequate export opportunity to make it attractive for them; and (ii) whether zero tariff on some products in the list will expose their domestic production to grave risk. A developing country may consider joining this exercise only if: (i) the list contains products of export interest to it; and (ii) the list does not contain such products, duty-free import of which may damage its critical domestic production.

Considering the sensitive nature of this exercise, it is desirable for the developing countries to ensure that participation is on a voluntary basis. Of course, when the negotiations are finalized, the benefit of zero duty on these products will be available to all the Members through the operation of the MFN principle, irrespective of whether or not they have reduced their own tariffs on these products to zero.

## *EROSION OF PREFERENCES*

An effective method should be worked out to address the problem of erosion of trade preferences for the developing countries. It will be helpful if, as a first step, the developing countries consider and discuss this matter among themselves to work out possible solutions. For example, in the case of preferences which will remain after these negotiations, it should be examined whether tight rules of origin would reduce the effective benefits to the developing countries. If so, improvements in the rules of origin should be suggested. Besides, the assistance of international financial institutions should be sought for improving the supply capacity and competitiveness of the developing countries which are adversely affected by the erosion of preferences.

### *NON-TARIFF BARRIERS*

Tariffs are only part of the problem in the area of market access. The other important part is non-tariff barriers and the developing countries are often the main victims here. Hence it is important for the developing countries to have an effective mechanism to solve this problem along with the tariff-reduction exercise. So far, the trend has been that the issue of NTBs is left as a residual topic in the NAMA negotiations, with central attention being given to tariffs. Since both tariffs and NTBs affect market access, however, it is necessary to have a clear parallelism in handling these two matters in the NAMA negotiations.

The WTO Secretariat has compiled a list of NTBs based on the notifications of Members. These are contained in documents TN/MA/S/5 of 11 September 2002, TN/MA/S/5/Rev.1 of 28 November 2003, TN/MA/W/25/Add.1 of 13 May 2003, TN/MA/W/25/Add.2 of 27 June 2003, TN/MA/W/46 of 26 November 2003, TN/MA/W/46/Add.1 of 4 March 2004 and TN/MA/W/46/Add.3 of 28 May 2004. These documents give the types of measures and the procedures applied. They can be a good guide to address the problem of NTBs.

A mechanism will need to be established to ensure parallelism in tackling NTBs and tariff reduction. The NAMA negotiating group should engage itself in this exercise. The best option is to have negotiations on NTBs conducted in this group. If, however, it is considered more convenient and efficient to handle different types of NTBs in different WTO bodies, the central control and monitoring of progress should still be in the hands of the NAMA group. These WTO bodies should meet in special sessions to handle the negotiations on NTBs, as is the case in many other bodies handling the current negotiations, e.g., special sessions of the Agriculture Committee, Council for Trade in Services, etc. Reports of the results of the negotiations should be made available to the NAMA group in each of its sessions. There should be a standing agenda item for this purpose. A decision may be taken in the General Council to consider these items in the special sessions of these bodies.

An initial exercise should be to list the types of NTBs and the procedures that need to be improved/modified. This listing will vary in content based on the interests of Members. In preparing such lists, the developing countries should keep their own interests and experience in view. Then they may prepare their suggestions for improvement/modification.

The NAMA group should be responsible for finalizing the decisions based on the results of the negotiations in the various WTO bodies.

### *DEVELOPING COUNTRIES' INITIATIVE*

To guide the negotiations along a course suitable to the developing countries, it is necessary for these countries to prepare consolidated specific proposals in various areas, like coverage, tariff-reduction formula for developed countries, tariff-reduction method for developing countries, sectoral approach, NTBs, base year, implementation period, erosion of preferences, etc. Already the developing countries have submitted a number of papers, as mentioned earlier. What is needed now is to consolidate them and put them under these specific headings for the negotiations. The developed countries are likely to suggest working on the basis of Annex B; hence it is necessary for the developing countries to prepare their own consolidated proposals and guide the negotiations towards their proposals in an alternative format.[13]

# Chapter 4

# TRADE FACILITATION

## BACKGROUND

THE decision on trade facilitation contained in Annex D to the July 04 decision was preceded by a serious controversy that had taken root as far back as the first WTO Ministerial Conference in Singapore in 1996. The major developed countries, particularly the EU, had proposed that negotiations should be launched in the WTO on the subjects of investment, competition policy, transparency in government procurement and trade facilitation. These four new subjects are collectively called the "Singapore issues" in WTO parlance. A large number of the developing countries were, however, opposed to expanding the scope of the WTO by entering into these new areas. In fact, they did not want to have any multilateral discipline in these areas at all. Further, they were particularly opposed to having negotiations in these areas in the WTO. They felt that it would be against their development interests, as multilateral agreements in these areas in the WTO would curtail their development options. Prompted by these considerations, they resolutely opposed the moves of the major developed countries. A large number of non-governmental organizations (NGOs), from both the developed and developing countries, also felt that bringing these subjects into the WTO framework of discipline would be a retrograde step. They mobilized public opinion in the developed and developing countries against this move.

These subjects continued to vitiate the atmosphere in the WTO right up to the Cancun Ministerial Conference and even thereafter. Finally, the developed countries sensed that they could not have it all their own way. An agreement was reached in the meeting of the General Council in July 2004 whereby it was decided to start negotiations to draw up an agreement in the area of trade facilitation but drop the other three subjects from the negotiating agenda of the Doha Work Programme.

## FRAMEWORK

The framework for the work in the area of trade facilitation is contained in Annex D to the July 04 decision (henceforward called Annex D in this chapter). It calls for negotiations which aim to "clarify and improve relevant aspects of Articles V, VIII and X of the GATT 1994 with a view to further expediting the movement, release and clearance of goods, including goods in transit" (para 1 of Annex D; hereafter the paragraph numbers in this chapter will refer to those in Annex D, except where specified otherwise).

The task is thus defined only in broad terms. The field is wide open at present. The coverage of the subjects of the negotiations will depend a lot on the proposals to be submitted by Members. Since this subject has been brought onto the agenda of negotiations at the persistent demand of the major developed countries, particularly the EU, some idea can be formed about the coverage proposals on the basis of their submissions and statements.

Firstly, however, it may be relevant to recapitulate the main contents of the three articles of the GATT 1994 referred to in paragraph 1.

Article V is about freedom of transit of goods. The relevant provision for our current consideration is that goods in transit through a country must not be subject to unnecessary delays and restrictions and must be exempt from customs duties. However, the transit country may require that the goods enter at the proper custom house and it may also formulate and apply customs laws and regulations which the goods in transit have to follow. Further, the transit country may also levy charges for transportation or those commensurate with administrative expenses or for the cost of services rendered.

In Article VIII, three provisions are relevant for the current exercise: (i) the fees and charges in connection with import and export (e.g., customs fees beyond the tariff) must be limited to the cost of services; (ii) there is a need to minimize the incidence and complexity of import and export formalities; and (iii) there is a need also for decreasing and simplifying import and export documentation requirements.

The relevant provisions of Article X are in two parts, one relating to publication and transparency and the other to the administration of laws. The two relevant provisions are: (i) laws, regulations and decisions relating to import and export must be published promptly in such a manner as to enable the governments and traders to become acquainted with them; and (ii) the laws relating to trade must be administered in a uniform, impartial and reasonable manner and there must be provision for judicial or quasi-judicial review of administrative decisions.

The stage is thus set for proposals to be made for clarifications and improvements of the aspects of these provisions that Members consider necessary.

There is an important provision in paragraph 6 that "implementation (by a developing- or least-developed-country Member) will not be required" where the "required support and assistance for (implementation) infrastructure is not forthcoming (from developed-country Members) and where a developing or least-developed Member continues to lack the necessary capacity." Here the reference is to the need for development of infrastructure for implementation of any resulting commitments. The developed-country Members are required to "make every effort to ensure support and assistance" (para 6).

## RANGE OF OPTIONS

Since the points of negotiations are given only in broad terms, as mentioned above, there is enough flexibility for keeping the negotiations limited in scope or making them wide-ranging. As this subject has remained controversial along with the other Singapore issues, the proponents have not expressed in detail what their proposals are. But some of the statements of the major developed countries from time to time give some indication of their objective at least in one area, viz., Article VIII. They may aim at relaxation of the customs procedures in the developing countries for clearance of imported goods. They may also try to press for some sort of harmonization in the rules for customs clearance and persuade the developing countries to adopt the procedures used in the major developed countries.

An important point in the range of options in this area is the nature of the outcome of the negotiations. Referring to the negotiations, footnote 1 in paragraph 1 says: "It is understood that this is without prejudice to the possible format of the final result of the negotiations and would allow consideration of various forms of outcomes". This is perhaps in recognition of the persistent argument of the developing countries that an agreement with technically enforceable provisions like those in the existing WTO agreements will not be appropriate in this area. They have from time to time strongly suggested that the result of the negotiations, if any, in this area should be in the nature of guidelines and not enforceable obligations.

With this footnote in place, the array of options ranges from having an agreement that is enforceable through the Dispute Settlement Understanding of the WTO to a result that is in the form of guidelines and excludes the application of the Dispute Settlement Understanding.

## SUGGESTIONS: WHAT SHOULD BE DONE?

Any harmonization of rules and practices in this area may create problems for the developing countries, as they will find it difficult to adopt the practices prevalent in the developed countries. For example, many developed countries examine only a small percentage of the arriving cargo at their customs point, selecting them on a sample basis. This practice may suit them, but it may not suit the developing countries, where there is much greater concern over leakage of customs revenue. The apprehension arises mainly because of the possibility of corruption in the system and the conduct of importers. Hence much greater coverage of inspection may be necessary in the developing countries.

Similarly, with regard to documentation requirements, there may be difficulty in copying the practices of the major developed countries, which have much higher sophistication and resources available in their system.

Of course, the developing countries should in any case strive to remove/reduce delays in the customs process and reduce the requirements of documentation. With this aim in view, they may study the processes followed in the developed countries and try to adopt as much as is suitable to them and as is possible within the constraints of their limited resources of trained personnel and finances. They could even do it on an experimental basis.

Considering all this, the following approaches may be appropriate for the developing countries:

(i) The scope of the exercise should be limited in coverage. Hence it will be necessary to examine the proposals of the proponents very closely.
(ii) Any new process emerging out of the negotiations should not be such as to add an unduly heavy burden on the administrative structure and finances of the developing countries. Close contact with the domestic administrative agencies working on the ground in these areas will be necessary at all stages of the negotiations, so that only practical and feasible new processes are introduced.
(iii) The results of the negotiations should be in the nature of guidelines and not rights and obligations which are enforceable through the Dispute Settlement Understanding process of the WTO.
(iv) In case any commitments are involved in the resulting agreement, it is necessary to include the provisions of paragraph 6 clearly in the agreement that free the developing countries, including the LDCs, from the obligation of implementation in the absence of adequate support and assistance from the developed countries in the development of their infrastructure.

# Chapter 5

# SERVICES

## BACKGROUND

THE WTO agreement on services, called the General Agreement on Trade in Services (GATS), is about liberalization of the entry of foreign services and foreign service providers into a country. Clearly it is for the benefit of the countries that have the capacity to supply services to other countries. As the developing countries do not generally have much supply capacity in this area, their prospect of benefiting from the GATS process is limited. To that extent, the agreement is almost totally one-sided. Further, some specific services sectors, particularly financial services and telecommunication services, were taken up for special negotiations on liberalization and agreements were reached for liberalization in these areas. As very few developing countries have any supply capacity at all in these sectors, these sectoral agreements added to the imbalance in the area of services. One aspect of services where several developing countries do have supply prospects is the provision of services by the movement of persons, technically called "Mode 4" of supply of service. But the major developed countries have hesitated in undertaking commitments on liberalization in this area on the ground that it relates to immigration policy. Thus the developing countries have effectively been left without benefits under the GATS.

Now a new round of negotiations has started for further liberalization of services trade under the Doha Work Programme. The major developed countries are pushing for further liberalization in the developing countries. The developing countries, on the other hand, are asking for liberalization in the areas where they may have prospects in the developed countries. We have to consider the current negotiations on services in this context.

## FRAMEWORK

There are three parallel tracks of ongoing negotiations in the area of services: (i) for specific commitments in various services sectors through the request-offer route; (ii) for working out rules on subsidies, safeguards and government procurement and disciplines on measures relating to qualification requirements and procedures, technical standards and licensing requirements; and (iii) for effective implementation of some important provisions of the GATS relating to the developing countries.

The framework for these negotiations is in the WTO document S/L/93 of 29 March 2001 entitled "Guidelines and Procedures for the Negotiations on Trade in Services" (reproduced in Annex 3 of this book) (henceforth called the Guidelines in this chapter) and in various relevant articles of the GATS.

The first track of the negotiations is guided by paragraph 11 of the Guidelines (henceforth the paragraph numbers in this chapter will refer to those in the Guidelines, except if specified otherwise), which says that the negotiations for liberalization (i.e., for specific commitments) will be mainly through the request-offer approach. Bilateral, plurilateral and multilateral negotiations are envisaged for this purpose. Regarding the developing countries, the Guidelines say, in consonance with Article XIX.2 and Article IV of the GATS (henceforth article numbers in this chapter will refer to those in the GATS, except if otherwise specified): "There shall be appropriate flexibility for individual developing country Members for opening fewer sectors, liberalizing fewer types of transactions, progressively extending market access in line with their development situation and, when making access to their markets available to foreign service suppliers, attaching to such access conditions aimed at achieving the objectives referred to in Article IV" (para 12).

The second track of the negotiations, i.e., those for rules in the areas of subsidies, safeguards and government procurement, is being conducted as required respectively in Articles XV, X and XIII. These articles prescribe that there shall be negotiations in these areas. Further, Article VI.4 requires that disciplines, as necessary, may be developed to ensure that "measures relating to qualification requirements and procedures, technical standards and licensing requirements do not constitute unnecessary barriers to trade in services".

The Guidelines lay down a time frame for completion of these negotiations: on safeguards (Article X) by 15 March 2002, as fixed earlier by the WTO Council for Trade in Services, and on the three other areas, i.e., Articles XV, XIII and VI.4, prior to the conclusion of the negotiations on specific commitments (para 7). Thus the Guidelines clearly recognize a link between the specific sectoral commitments and the disciplines under these articles, and establish a sequential priority that the negotiations on these disciplines must be completed before those on specific commitments.

The third track of negotiations is guided by paragraphs 14 and 15, which call for an assessment from time to time of the implementation of Articles IV and XIX.2. Article IV requires that the increasing participation of the developing countries in world trade shall be facilitated through specific commitments by different Members relating to the strengthening of the domestic services capacity of the developing countries, improvement of their access to distribution channels and information networks, and liberalization of market access in sectors and modes of supply of export interest to the developing countries. Article XIX.2 stipulates liberalization by developing countries of fewer types of transactions and in fewer sectors, and also envisages developing countries' attaching to their liberalization conditions aimed at achieving the objectives referred to in Article IV.

There is an important directive in the Guidelines that "negotiations shall be adjusted in the light of the results of the assessment" (para 14).

## DEVELOPING COUNTRIES' PROPOSALS AND CONCERNS

The developing countries have put forth a large number of proposals and comments in the course of the negotiations. Some of them have submitted offers and requests. Specific proposals and comments have been given by some developing countries in the negotiations on the rules. A large number of developing countries have given proposals on Articles IV and XIX.2 and on the provision of services by the movement of natural persons, i.e., on Mode 4 of service supply.

Pressure has been exerted on those countries that have not given offers so far to give their offers soon. But, as will be explained later, it is not obligatory for a country to give offers; this depends very much instead on the country's assessment of gains.

Negotiations are going on in the rules areas mainly on technical issues and clarifications. The trend shows that the progress is slow. Consideration of the development aspects as in Articles IV and XIX.2 has been initiated at the instance of the developing countries, but without much progress.

A large number of developing countries have expressed dissatisfaction with the offers given by the developed countries. They say that the developed countries are not making meaningful offers in the sectors and modes of interest to the developing countries. For example, provision of service by the movement of the service provider to the country where the service is to be provided (Mode 4) is an important area for the developing countries and they have repeatedly been asking for commitments from the developed countries to ease restrictions on the movement of natural persons for this purpose to the developed countries. The developing countries have expressed disappointment that the preliminary offers of the developed countries do not include this item in any effective way.

Rather, the commitments of the developed countries on Mode 4 are mainly related to the movement of persons connected with "commercial presence". ("Commercial presence" in GATS parlance refers to the supply of service through the setting up of a firm by a service provider of one country in another country.) Mainly it is the developed countries that have commercial presence abroad; thus these commitments are primarily for their own mutual benefit. The developing countries have specified that the developed countries should cover a wider range of service-provider categories and occupations for commitments on Mode 4 and expand the commitments relating to personnel delinked from commercial presence. Right now the commitments are mainly in respect of intra corporate transferees and business visitors; these should be expanded to include other categories like contractual service suppliers and independent service providers.

In the negotiations on rules also, the developing countries are dissatisfied with the slow progress in the area of safeguards. Some of them have presented detailed proposals and have responded to questions and comments, yet the negotiations are still dragging on. At the same time, some major developed countries are trying to push forward the negotiations in the area of government procurement where they have a keen interest, as they wish to expand their market access in the developing countries.

On the development parameters contained in Articles IV and XIX.2, though the developing countries have made observations and given suggestions, there has been no serious engagement in the negotiations. The developed countries do not appear to have given attention to this matter so far.

## SUGGESTIONS: WHAT SHOULD BE DONE?

### *BACKGROUND AND IMPLICATIONS*

As explained earlier, the very existence of an agreement like the GATS is an example of the imbalance in the WTO, because this agreement is centred around expansion of market access and there is a vast differential in supply capacity between the developed countries and the developing countries in services. The imbalance has been aggravated by accelerated and special negotiations and agreements in certain specific services sectors, like financial services and telecommunication services, where the developed countries have a far superior advantage in supply capacity.

Some measure of balance was sought to be brought into the GATS by stipulating special provisions for the benefit and safeguard of the developing countries, particularly in Articles IV and XIX.2. But these provisions have either been ignored, as in the case of the latter, or simply not been acted on, as in the case of the former.

Over the years of operation of the agreement, the developing countries have tried to explore opportunities for service export and identified certain areas. But in spite of their expressions of concern and proposals, they have not succeeded so far in making the developed countries move in a positive direction in these areas, as has been discussed above. Therefore the developing countries now have to decide on their moves and strategies in the light of the structural imbalances in the GATS and their experience in the negotiations thus far.

## *SPECIFIC COMMITMENTS*[14]

The current exercise in this negotiating track involves the submission of offers and requests. Some Members have already done so. Based on the response of the other Members, they will then be expected to submit revised offers. And there may be bilateral and plurilateral negotiations for exchanges of concessions across different services sectors. In this process, the following relevant and important points should be taken into account:

(i) Those developing countries that do not expect to gain market access for their services in other countries need not submit any offers. The request-offer method of negotiations is an exercise in direct reciprocity. Thus a country that does not expect to "gain" need not "give". Hence such developing countries need not get pushed by the momentum of the negotiating process and must not feel compelled to make any offers. Of course, a likely consequence is that they will be excluded from the bilateral/plurilateral negotiations to finalize the list of concessions by Members and work out relevant procedures. But as they do not expect any gain from such sectoral concessions anyway, they may have nothing to lose by such exclusion.

(ii) Those developing countries that do intend to make offers and get concessions from others in return should prepare their offers and revised offers and also decide on their approach for the bilateral/plurilateral negotiations. In this process the following considerations may be helpful to them, both while preparing their offer list and while engaging in the negotiations for give-and-take.

(a) A developing country should assess if there are sectors where it must not allow entry to foreign services. For example, there could be areas that are sensitive for security reasons or important for public-welfare reasons. A developing country may decide that there should be only domestic service providers in these areas. Based on this assessment, a "negative list" should be prepared where the country will not make any commitment for liberalization. The country will thus be clear on the sectors where no concession is to be given and it can then proceed to have constructive talks with other countries for give-and-take in other services sectors.

(b) It should prepare a "critical list" which includes services sectors that are critical to its economic development and where it is necessary to encourage domestic production of services. In these areas, even though the country may not stop the entry of foreign services altogether, it should still protect the domestic services against competition from the foreign services and service providers. Some examples of such sectors may be banking, telecommunication, etc. In these sectors, the objective of the country in the negotiations should be to impose stringent conditions on market entry and retain full flexibility to provide support to domestic services without extending it to foreign services, i.e., full flexibility regarding the discipline on national treatment. (Without such flexibility, the country would be obliged, under the national-treatment principle, to accord foreign services and service providers treatment that is no less favourable than that accorded to their domestic counterparts.)

(c) It should also prepare a "desirable import list" of sectors that are necessary and useful for its domestic production of goods and services and where there is little prospect of developing domestic supply capacity. Naturally, the country should be more willing in the negotiations to offer liberalization in these sectors, provided it gets commensurate offers from others in the sectors in which it has export interest.

The three lists suggested above should be for the internal use of the country and not for submission in the negotiations. These lists will guide the negotiators in the bilateral and plurilateral sectoral negotiations for specific commitments.

(iii) A request list should be prepared and, if already prepared, should be evaluated on the basis of the following considerations:

(a) The sectors and modes where the country has export capacity at present or where there is a potential for developing export capacity in the near future should be considered for inclusion.

(b) For these sectors, the country should collect information on the current restrictions and likely restrictions in the countries where there is potential for export. If there is no restriction or likely restriction on any of these sectors in a country, this sector should not be included in the request list for that country. It is to be understood that a request will have to be balanced by an offer at some stage. Thus if the opportunity for export in this sector already exists in that country and is not likely to be constrained, it is not prudent to make a request.

(iv) Negotiations for specific sectoral commitments should be across sectors. No individual sector should be selected for special treatment, as was done earlier in the case of financial services and telecommunication services, where the developing countries had little supply capacity. If the negotiations are conducted across sectors, it is more likely that there will be some sectors under negotiation in which the developing countries have export potential.

(v) In its request list, a developing country may also include a request for removal of some general constraints, like those on the entry of natural persons for providing services and those on qualification requirements and procedures, technical standards and licensing requirements as well as on recognition of qualifications and standards prevalent in the country. These may be the main barriers in the developed countries against the service exports of the developing countries; hence it may be desirable for the developing countries to give emphasis to them in their requests.

## *FORMULATION OF RULES AND DISCIPLINES*

(i) It is important for the developing countries to have an effective safeguard system in services, so that they can ensure protection to their domestic service providers against sudden imports. Specific proposals have already been submitted in this area, particularly by the ASEAN (Association of South-East Asian Nations) countries. Several other developing countries have supported the proposals. The major developed countries may not like to have an effective safeguard system in place, as they would prefer totally unhindered entry of their services into the developing countries. The negotiations seem to have got mired in technical details and it is necessary to kickstart progress here. It is relevant in this connection to remind the negotiating group that the Guidelines make it mandatory to complete the negotiations on the rules before completing those on specific sectoral commitments.

(ii) In the area of subsidies, it is vital for the developing countries to retain the flexibility to give subsidies for the development and export of their services because of the initial handicaps of their services sectors in facing international competition. The developed countries would need to appreciate the special situation of the developing countries in this regard.
In this area, it is important to note the difference between the current provisions in the goods sector and in the services sector. Providing domestic subsidies in the goods sector is not considered to violate the principle of national treatment as there is an exception in Article III.8 of the GATT 1994, but there is no such general exception in the GATS. Hence it should be ensured that the developing countries include this exception under Article XVII of the GATS in all sectors that they include in their schedules of sectoral commitments. Alternatively, there may be a general exception in the GATS along the lines of Article III.8 of the GATT 1994.

(iii) It is anticipated that the major developed countries may like to push for a liberal agreement in the area of government procurement. It is important to work for a balanced result that does not unduly constrain the flexibility of the developing countries in giving reasonable preferences to their domestic suppliers. Any concession in this area from the developing countries' side should be given only if they are satisfied that they would get meaningful market access in the developed countries' government procurement in return. This will require a close examination of the possible opportunities for providing services for government use in the developed countries. The opportunities are to be assessed on the basis of the availability of such a market in the developed country as well as the supply capacity of the developing country.

(iv) The negotiations on developing disciplines for qualifications, standards and licensing are very important for the developing countries. These are intimately linked with market access. A developing country may get full access commitment in a sector in a developed country and yet may not enjoy any effective access because of stringent qualifications, standards and licensing requirements. These are the services-sector counterparts of the NTBs in the goods sector. Hence progress in negotiations in this area should go in step with the negotiations on specific sectoral commitments.

## *CONSIDERATION OF ARTICLES IV AND XIX.2*

A large number of developing countries have combined to submit proposals in this area. They have also submitted a critical assessment of the offers of the developed countries in the context of these mandatory provisions. However, they do not appear to have made any effective impact so far on the approach of the developed countries. But it is necessary for the developing countries to continue with their effort; otherwise, whatever possibility of slight gains there is in the GATS framework would be totally lost.

## *STRATEGIC ADVANTAGES AND APPROACHES*

The developing countries do possess some strategic advantages in the services negotiations and they should fully utilize them.

Firstly, it should be borne in mind that the developed countries introduced this subject in the WTO framework mainly to obtain concessions from the developing countries. If they had intended to establish an inter-developed-country framework, they could have easily done so in the OECD (Organization for Economic Cooperation and Development) setup. As it is the developing countries which are the main targets, they are exposed to risks and are put on the defensive. But this situation also gives them a strategic advantage. Any concession from the side of the developing countries can be obtained only if these countries are willing to make those concessions. And they can decide not to give concessions, except if their objectives, priorities and proposals are substantially accepted. It is to be noted that a stalemate in this area will be more to the disadvantage of the developed countries than the developing countries. Hence if the developing countries are steadfast in their proposals and approaches, the initiative in these negotiations will in fact be in their hands rather than in the hands of the developed countries.

Secondly, many provisions of the Guidelines are helpful to them in this regard. Two of these provisions are particularly important and effective:

(i) The negotiations on rules are to be completed before the conclusion of the negotiations on specific commitments (para 7). A parallelism in the progress in these two tracks of negotiations is thereby indicated. Towards this end, the developing countries may insist on a parallel review of progress in the Special Sessions of the WTO Council for Trade in Services with the objective of having comparable progress in both tracks.

(ii) Paragraph 14 asks for mandatory adjustment of the negotiations from time to time after an assessment is undertaken with reference to the objectives of the GATS, in particular Article IV. This gives the developing countries a mandate to seek an adjustment in the negotiations if they find at some stage that the objectives are not being fulfilled for diverse reasons, including because of pressures from the major developed countries.

These strategic advantages can be put to good use, particularly if the developing countries, or at least a large number of them, act together. Already many of them have come together to place proposals in the negotiations.

# Chapter 6

# IMPLEMENTATION ISSUES

## BACKGROUND

SHORTLY after the coming into force of the WTO agreements, the developing countries became aware of several problems with the implementation of these agreements. They raised these issues at the Singapore Ministerial Conference in 1996 and again at the Geneva Ministerial Conference in 1998. The Ministerial Declarations issued by these conferences referred to these problems of the developing countries but there was no effective solution. By then the developing countries had experienced a very large number of implementation problems and they started listing them. Finally, in the process of preparation for the Seattle Ministerial Conference in 1999, they prepared a consolidated list of nearly 100 of these "implementation issues". After some problems, they succeeded in getting them included in the General Council Chairman's text for that conference. This gave a formal status to these issues as a part of the agenda of the Ministerial Conference. However, that conference collapsed in disagreement; thus no decision could be taken on these issues too. But they remained on the WTO agenda.

The developing countries persisted with them in the preparatory process for the Doha Ministerial Conference in 2001 and also during the conference itself. Finally, specific decisions were taken on these issues in the Doha Ministerial Declaration. And there was also a clarification made through a statement by the Chairman of the conference. These constitute the basis for the negotiations on these issues as a part of the Doha Work Programme.

## FRAMEWORK

The framework is basically provided by paragraph 12 of the Doha Declaration, which adopted a decision of the General Council contained in document WT/MIN(01)/17 (reproduced in Annex 4 of this book) and gave directions on how to address the unresolved implementation issues. In this document, the General Council had taken specific decisions of a final nature only on three issues: (i) in respect of the Agreements on the Application of Sanitary and Phytosanitary (SPS) Measures and on Technical Barriers to Trade, it specified "a reasonable interval" between the publication of a measure or a standard and its coming into force; (ii) in respect of the Agreement on the Application of SPS Measures, it specified "longer time-frames for compliance" with the measures in respect of products of interest to the developing countries; and (iii) with regard to the Agreement on Subsidies and Countervailing Measures, it specified the criteria for exclusion and re-inclusion of developing countries in a group of Members which were entitled to some concessions. In respect of the other implementation issues, the General Council gave directions to different WTO bodies for further action.

The Doha Declaration says in paragraph 12 that "negotiations on outstanding implementation issues shall be an integral part of the Work Programme we are establishing" (i.e., the Doha Work Programme).

A comprehensive ensemble of the implementation issues is contained in WT/MIN(01)/17 and in the WTO document JOB(01)/152/Rev.1 of 27 October 2001 entitled "Compilation of Outstanding Implementation Issues Raised by Members" (reproduced in Annex 5 of this book). Out of these, only three issues were finally settled by the General Council decision, as mentioned above. The others are outstanding issues and are thus to be addressed as decided in paragraph 12 of the Doha Declaration.

At the time of the Doha Ministerial Conference, some concerns arose that the text of paragraph 12 could give an impression that the only outstanding issues were those contained in the document JOB(01)/152/Rev.1, when in fact the issues contained in WT/MIN(01)/17, except for the three mentioned earlier, were also outstanding. To allay any such concerns, the Chairman of the conference gave a clarification in a statement in the conference. He said: "With regard to the outstanding implementation issues, I would like to recall the cover letter of 5 November 2001, sent to me by the Chairman of the General Council and the (WTO) Director General, which accompanied the draft decision on implementation. It states that the draft decision proposes immediate action on a number of implementation issues, and provides that remaining issues, which include those referred to WTO bodies as well as those listed in their completion (compilation) will be addressed in the course of the future work programme in accordance with paragraph 12 of the draft ministerial declaration". This removes all uncertainties about what the outstanding issues to be addressed are. All the issues, i.e., those listed in JOB(01)/152/Rev.1 and also those sent to various WTO bodies and negotiating groups as recommended by the Chairman of the General Council and decided in the conference in WT/MIN(01)/17, constitute the outstanding issues to be addressed in the current negotiations.

The means of handling these issues mentioned in the Doha Declaration are: (i) addressing them under specific mandates of negotiation if they are covered by such mandate; and (ii) addressing the others in the relevant WTO bodies as a matter of priority. Further, paragraph 12 says: "... (except for the Dispute Settlement Understanding negotiations) agreements reached at an early stage in these negotiations shall be treated in accordance with the provisions of paragraph 47 below". Paragraph 47 of the Doha Declaration says: "... the outcome of the negotiations shall be treated as parts of a single undertaking. However, agreements reached at an early stage may be implemented on a provisional basis or a definitive basis. Early agreements shall be taken into account in assessing the overall balance of the negotiations".

Some developed countries have started raising doubts as to whether all the outstanding issues mentioned above will be subject to negotiations. In fact, there is no cause for doubt in this regard. The Chairman's statement makes it clear that all the unsolved issues are outstanding issues. Then, paragraph 12 of the Doha Declaration says: "We agree that negotiations on the outstanding implementation issues shall be an integral part of the Work Programme we are establishing ..." Further, paragraph 12 also makes the negotiations on outstanding issues a part of the "single undertaking" in the negotiations under the Doha Work Programme. All this leaves no scope for doubt that all these outstanding issues are to be covered by the negotiations.

As the negotiations on the outstanding implementation issues are a part of the single undertaking in the Doha Work Programme negotiations, these issues cannot be left behind. They must be settled before the end of the negotiations; otherwise, the overall balance of the negotiations cannot be assessed.[15]

## PROGRESS

The progress in the negotiations on the implementation issues has been very tardy. The developing countries got too involved with the subjects of agriculture, NAMA and Singapore issues in the preparations for the Cancun Ministerial Conference and thereafter. They have not been able to pursue the implementation issues in the negotiations, although they were the proponents of the issues and they are the Members most interested in them. As they have not been able to spend time on and devote attention to this subject for some time, there has been inadequate progress.

## SUGGESTIONS: WHAT SHOULD BE DONE?

It is important for the developing countries to bring this subject to centrestage once again, as they had done on the way to Seattle and then in Doha. They have already done a lot of work in this area and their proposals are very specific. They may not need much additional effort and resources to pursue this subject in the negotiations.

They also have the advantage of the framework which says that the results of the negotiations in this area will be a part of the single undertaking. As such, they must be completed along with the negotiations in the other areas. In fact, as these issues relate to problems with the existing WTO agreements, they should have priority over negotiations that are working on new agreements.

The implementation issues that are covered by the mandated negotiations in the Doha Declaration will automatically be a part of the negotiations on that particular subject. The others that are being addressed by different WTO bodies will need to be specially attended to. The Doha Declaration asks for these issues to be addressed "as a matter of priority". One way may be to consider these subjects in special sessions of these respective bodies so that concentrated and exclusive attention is devoted to these issues. The special sessions of these bodies should send status reports to the General Council/Trade Negotiations Committee so that the progress is monitored along with the progress in other areas of the negotiations.

# Chapter 7

# SUBSIDIES, ANTI-DUMPING, RTAs, DSU

## FRAMEWORK

THE framework for negotiations in the areas of subsidies and anti-dumping is contained in paragraph 28, in the area of regional trade agreements (RTAs) in paragraph 29 and in the area of the Dispute Settlement Understanding (DSU) in paragraph 30 of the Doha Declaration. The objective of the negotiations is to have clarifications and improvements in the WTO rules in these areas.

Clarification normally involves removing doubts and confusion in the rules and selecting preferred courses if several alternatives are admissible under a particular provision of an agreement. It is a process of specifying the manner of implementation of a provision of an agreement without amending it. It may be desirable, for instance, to bring in some uniformity of practice or procedure when the rules permit a range of options. Improvement, on the other hand, may involve amendment. However, "improving the discipline" does not necessarily mean making the discipline more stringent; it could also involve making the discipline less stringent. The latter option may be called for when there is unnecessary or improper stringency in the discipline.

## PROPOSALS

The developing countries have already given several proposals in these areas. In fact, a large number of proposals had been covered while listing out the implementation issues. Then there were several additional ones put forward during the course of the work of this negotiating group. Some of the proposals have been persistently pursued by the developing countries in the negotiations. There may be further new proposals in the future course of the negotiations. Since the list of existing proposals is a long one, it may not be practical to enumerate them here. However, some of the critical issues that have repeatedly irked the developing countries in the recent past and some others that are urgent are explained in the next section.

## SUGGESTIONS: WHAT SHOULD BE DONE?

In these four areas, it may be important for the developing countries to pursue the following proposals.

### *SUBSIDIES*

(i) Given that the "needs and interests" of the developing countries have been placed "at the heart of the Work Programme" in paragraph 2 of the Doha Declaration, the subsidies of the developing countries for upgradation of technology and diversification of the industrial base should be made "non-actionable", i.e., not subjected to countervailing duties or relief through the dispute settlement process of the WTO. It may be recalled that the Agreement on Subsidies and Countervailing Measures includes provisions (now lapsed since 1 January 2000) that make subsidies for research and development, environmental adaptation and regional development, which are normally prevalent in the developed countries, non-actionable (the validity of these provisions continued for five years of the implementation of the agreement and was not renewed thereafter).

(ii) Import-substitution subsidies should be admissible in the developing countries. If used in a progressive and dynamic manner, they can be a useful instrument for industrial expansion and upgradation in these countries.

(iii) In the calculation of subsidy margins, the onus should be on the country imposing the countervailing duty to include only those payments that accrue as benefits "in the production of the export product". It must make a reasoned decision to include a particular amount in the calculation of subsidy.

(iv) The amount of the countervailing duty should be limited to the subsidy margin or injury margin, whichever is lower. This "lesser duty" provision is common to both subsidies and anti-dumping, but it is generally ignored by the major developed countries in implementation. They do determine the existence of injury, which is mandatory, but do not determine or make public the determination of the "injury margin", i.e., the level of duty that would remove the injury. The Agreement on Subsidies and Countervailing Measures makes such determination "desirable"; hence it is argued that it is not mandatory. There is a need to make it mandatory. In any case, even now the legality of not following the "lesser duty" provision is doubtful. Article 15.5 of the Agreement on Subsidies and Countervailing Measures says "it must be demonstrated that the subsidized imports are, through the effects of subsidies, causing injury". Hence imposition of even a portion of the countervailing duty without the existence of injury is illegal. And that is precisely what happens when the amount of the imposed duty is higher than the injury margin.

There is thus a need for clarification in the agreement that the countervailing duty must be limited to the subsidy margin or injury margin, whichever is lower.

### *ANTI-DUMPING*

(i) The "lesser duty" rule, as explained above in the case of subsidies, is also valid for anti-dumping duties; thus the current practice of the major developed countries in ignoring it needs to be redressed. The relevant provisions in the Anti-dumping Agreement are similar to those in the Agreement on Subsidies and Countervailing Measures that have been explained above; hence similar action is needed here as well.

(ii) There are *de minimis* levels for dumping margin (2 percent) and dumped volume (3 percent of the import of the product in the country) for general use. There is no enhanced *de minimis* provision for the developing countries, however. Considering that they have been subjected to great harassment in the form of repeated anti-dumping investigations and anti-dumping duties, it appears desirable to allow substantially raised *de minimis* levels for the developing countries' exports, in respect of both the dumping margin and dumped volume.

(iii) There is a need to improve the operation of the "sunset clause", which prescribes the termination of an anti-dumping duty at the end of five years (Article 11.3 of the Anti-dumping Agreement). The termination is made mandatory, but there is a loophole that provides an escape route for the countries which impose anti-dumping duties. The relevant provision is: "any anti-dumping duty shall be terminated on a date not later than five years from its imposition ... unless the authorities determine … that the expiry of the duty would be likely to lead to continuation or recurrence of dumping and injury". The processes followed in the major developed countries are heavily weighted towards continuation of the duty beyond the five years. This provision should thus be modified to require a definitive end to the duty at the end of five years. If the situation so demands, a fresh determination of dumping and resulting injury may be made at the end of the five years, and all the processes of levying a new duty may have to be followed.

### *RTAs*

(i) Article XXIV of the GATT 1994 recognizes that "the purpose of a customs union or a free trade area should be to facilitate trade between the constituent territories and not to raise barriers to the trade of other contracting parties with such territories". Further, it says that "the duties and other regulations of commerce imposed at the institution of any such union or agreement in respect of trade with contracting parties not parties to such union or agreement shall not on the whole be higher or more restrictive than the general incidence of the duties and regulations of commerce applicable in the constituent territories prior to the formation of such union or adoption of such interim agreement ..." In the case of the formation of a customs union or free trade area among developed countries, the burden of proof should be on the constituent developed countries to demonstrate that the developing countries will not face higher barriers or restrictions.

(ii) To facilitate and encourage the formation of customs unions or free trade areas among the developing countries, the requirement in Article XXIV.8 of elimination of duties and restrictions in respect of "substantially all the trade between the constituent territories" should be relaxed.

### *DSU*

The Dispute Settlement Understanding is a WTO agreement which sets rules and procedures governing the resolution of trade disputes between Member countries. Under this dispute settlement process, a panel of experts may be established to examine a complaint and give its finding and recommendation on the complaint, while any party to the dispute which is not satisfied with the panel's finding and recommendation may lodge an appeal with the WTO Appellate Body.

The DSU was considered to be the major achievement of the Uruguay Round, but the experience of its operation shows that it needs much improvement. Though conscious of this, the developing countries are reluctant to reopen this agreement, perhaps because they feel that it has been providing them some protection in spite of its deficiencies. Nevertheless, even without amending the agreement, certain improvements can be made simply by means of taking a decision in the Ministerial Conference or even in the General Council. Improvements of this type on two aspects are suggested below.

(i) It has been noticed that the dispute settlement panels and the Appellate Body are undertaking the task of making major interpretations of some of the basic provisions in the WTO agreements. This may modify the balance of rights and obligations which had been arrived at during the Uruguay Round negotiations. Usually relief against such a problem would be through the legislative route by way of an amendment or authoritative interpretation of the agreements concerned. But it is difficult to take this course in the context of the decision-making process in the WTO. Hence it is necessary to prevent or discourage the panels and Appellate Body from giving major interpretations. For example, when a provision of a WTO agreement confers a right and another provision takes away or restricts this right, the panels and Appellate Body have developed the practice of deciding which of the two provisions would prevail. Each agreement of the WTO is a result of negotiations among sovereign governments and, as such, it should be beyond the role of the panels and Appellate Body to modify the operation of the agreement. It is desirable that the Ministerial Conference or the General Council give formal guidance to the panels and Appellate Body that they should refrain from weighing between two provisions, particularly of two separate agreements, when they come to the conclusion that the two provisions have opposite or substantially different content in respect of the issue in dispute.

(ii) The DSU process is very costly and thus the developing countries often hesitate to start a formal dispute settlement process. This results in an imbalance between developed and developing countries in the capacity to enforce their rights and obligations. It can be remedied by a provision of financial compensation as cost of the process to a developing-country disputant when the other party in the dispute is a developed country and the stand of the developing country has been upheld by the panel/Appellate Body. The panel/Appellate Body may be authorized to assess the cost and grant it in such cases.

# Chapter 8

# ENVIRONMENT

## FRAMEWORK

THE negotiations in the area of the environment are guided by paragraphs 31 and 32 of the Doha Declaration. The main relevant contents are the following:

(i) There will be negotiations on:
   (a) the relationship between the WTO rules and the provisions of multilateral environmental agreements (MEAs);
   (b) reduction/elimination of tariffs and NTBs on "environmental goods and services."

(ii) Particular attention will be given to:
   (a) the effects of environmental measures on market access;
   (b) the relevant provisions of the Agreement on Trade-Related Aspects of Intellectual Property Rights (TRIPS);
   (c) labelling requirements for environmental purposes.

The work has started in these areas, but there has been no appreciable progress towards an agreement. Hence there are still wide options for the developing countries to pursue their objectives and approaches in this area.

## SUGGESTIONS: WHAT SHOULD BE DONE?[16]

The following suggestions are relevant for the developing countries in the background of the passage of this subject in the WTO.

(i) While acting on trade-restrictive measures in accordance with the MEAs, the disciplines of the WTO must be respected and followed. In individual cases of conflict or difference between the respective provisions of these two sets of agreements, the two inter-governmental institutions (i.e., the WTO and the organization administering the particular MEA) should jointly address the matter through a mechanism to be evolved by them. One way may be to refer the matter to the UN for reconciliation.

(ii) "Environmental goods and services" should be defined. There can be two types of criteria, viz.: (i) goods that are produced in an environmentally friendly manner; and (ii) goods that support the production of environmentally friendly goods, e.g., appropriate machines, equipment, chemicals, etc.

The problem with the first criterion is that such a definition will formally recognize a distinction between goods which have the same contents and characteristics but are produced in different ways. Such a distinction will be based on what is technically called "unrelated" processes and production methods (PPMs) and has been consistently opposed by the developing countries because, apart from some systemic problems, it may be used by the major developed countries to justify trade restrictions. Such a definition will therefore not be proper for the developing countries in the long term.

On the basis of the second criterion, the negotiations for reduction/elimination of tariffs and NTBs on such goods should be held in the NAMA negotiating group and not in the negotiating group for environment. Generally the machines, equipment and chemicals of this type are produced by the developed countries. They should engage in negotiations in the NAMA group for these products along with other products and be prepared to offer concessions in return. It will be unfair and unbalanced to treat liberalization in these sectors separately, as the developing countries will then be expected to make all the concessions without getting any in return since they do not generally produce and export these products. In any case, as the NAMA group is the specialized group handling tariffs and NTBs, this subject should be handled there and not in the negotiating group for environment.

(iii) The WTO Secretariat has prepared a compilation of NTBs, as mentioned in the chapter on NAMA. It includes trade-restrictive environmental measures too. This list can facilitate consideration of the effects of environmental measures on market access.

(iv) Regarding the relevant provisions of the TRIPS Agreement, there may be proposals for: (a) qualifying the rights of patent holders in respect of machinery, equipment and chemicals that facilitate environmentally friendly production and practices; and (b) consideration of the linkage with the UN Convention on Biological Diversity, particularly in respect of Article 27.3(b) of the TRIPS Agreement regarding the patenting of plants and animals.

(v) Consideration of labelling requirements should give attention to the possible serious burden such requirements could impose on exporters from the developing countries.

# Chapter 9

# TRIPS

## FRAMEWORK

THE framework on TRIPS contained in paragraphs 17, 18 and 19 of the Doha Declaration is quite comprehensive. The essential elements are as follows:

(i) A separate declaration was adopted by the Doha Ministerial Conference (reproduced in Annex 6 of this book) relating to public health and compulsory licensing (using a patented product without the authorization of the patent holder), and the WTO's TRIPS Council was asked by the declaration to solve the problems involved in importing patented drugs in developing countries with inadequate manufacturing capacity where indigenous production through compulsory licensing would not be feasible.

(ii) Negotiations have been launched on establishing a multilateral system for notification and registration of geographical indications for wines and spirits.

(iii) Paragraph 19 makes reference to: (a) the review of Article 27.3(b) of the TRIPS Agreement; (b) the review under Article 71.1 of the implementation of the TRIPS Agreement; and (c) work under paragraph 12 of the Doha Declaration about the negotiations on the implementation issues. Then it goes on to ask for examination of: (a) the relationship between the TRIPS Agreement and the Convention on Biological Diversity; (b) protection of traditional knowledge and folklore; and (c) other relevant new developments raised by Members pursuant to the review under Article 71.1.

## SUGGESTIONS: WHAT SHOULD BE DONE?

On the matter of public health and compulsory licensing, intense negotiations resulted in an interim agreement on 30 August 2003 (reproduced in Annex 7 of this book). Under this agreement, a solution has been found to overcome the constraint the producing-exporting country faces in issuing a compulsory licence for the production of an affordable version of a patented drug to be exported to a developing country in need. The constraint arises because Article 31(f) of the TRIPS Agreement states that while a government can issue a compulsory licence for indigenous manufacture of a patented product, it must be on condition that the production will be predominantly for domestic use. This constraint has been provisionally waived under the interim agreement, thus enabling a developing country to use a compulsory licence to produce drugs for export to another developing country in need. Now a permanent solution in the form of an amendment to the TRIPS Agreement itself is under negotiation. All this has been possible because of the intense pressure exerted by the African countries, supported by a large number of NGOs of the developing countries and developed countries, in the context of problems faced by the African countries in obtaining drugs to treat serious diseases at reasonable prices.

Progress has also been made on the notification and registration of geographical indications of wines and spirits. But a related topic of expanding the geographical indications to some other products of interest to some developing countries has not made much headway.

There has been practically no progress on the other issues. The developing countries have also not been pursuing them with vigour. The reason may be that they have been too occupied with negotiations in other areas, particularly agriculture and NAMA. It may also be because some of them are hesitant in reopening the provisions of the TRIPS Agreement. They may be concerned that the agreement will become even more detrimental to their interests in the process.

An important point to be kept in mind in this connection is that the current negotiations provide an opportunity to the developing countries to clarify and improve some provisions of the TRIPS Agreement. If this opportunity is missed now, there may not be any chance of improvement for a long time to come. The developing countries have already included a number of proposals on the TRIPS Agreement, particularly on the patent regime, as part of the implementation issues. The framework described above gives them enough scope for working out solutions to the problems.

The following points may be of interest to the developing countries in pursuing the negotiations in the area of TRIPS:

(i) The developing countries have been proposing that plants and animals or their parts and essentially biological processes for the production of plants and animals should not be patented. Article 27.3(b) of the TRIPS Agreement gives discretion to a country to exclude them from patentability, but it does not prohibit a country from allowing them to be patented. In order to stop the patenting of these items altogether, this article will need to be amended to say so clearly.

(ii) Article 27.3 makes it compulsory for a country to provide for the patenting of micro-organisms. But this term is not defined. It should be clarified that this term does not include naturally occurring micro-organisms like naturally occurring bacteria, fungi, algae, protozoa or viruses. And patenting of naturally occurring micro-organisms should be prohibited.

(iii) It has often been observed that patents are claimed and granted on matters which are within the traditional knowledge of some community. A clear decision should be taken that patents must not be granted for a subject matter that has been available to the public in a country by means of use or written description or in any other manner.

(iv) It is necessary to stop the practice of what has been called biopiracy. The developing countries are the main victims and losers in this process, under which patents are claimed and granted for materials derived from the plants of a country. In many such cases, the country that is the source of the plant does not even know about the granting of the patent. Also, the economic benefits from the patent are not shared with that country. There should thus be a clear provision that the applicant for the patent must get the permission/consent of the country of origin of the plant from which the subject of the patent is derived. Also, there should be a provision for sharing the economic benefits with the country of origin of the plant.

(v) A review under Article 71.1 would bring to light the problems faced by the developing countries in respect of the workings of the patent regime. One example is the problem of the availability of drugs, which has been the subject matter of negotiations as mentioned above. There may be other similar problems. It is therefore advisable to start and complete the review quickly and bring the perceived problems before the current negotiations in order to arrive at a solution.

# Chapter 10

# TRADE, DEBT AND FINANCE

## FRAMEWORK

THE framework for the WTO's consideration of the relationship between trade, debt and finance is provided by paragraph 36 of the Doha Declaration. It asks for recommendations on steps to: (i) enhance the capacity of the multilateral trading system to contribute to a durable solution to the problem of external indebtedness of the developing countries; and (ii) strengthen the coherence of international trade and financial policies with a view to safeguarding the multilateral trading system from the effects of financial and monetary instability. Consideration of this matter has started and continued, but no conclusive results have been achieved so far.

## SUGGESTIONS: WHAT SHOULD BE DONE?

(i) The link between a durable solution to/easing of the external indebtedness of the developing countries and expanded access for their goods and services in the developed countries that are major markets should be explored and a set of recommendations may be worked out in this light. The recommendations within the remit of the WTO may focus on policies and measures in the major markets that can encourage the expansion of production and trade of the developing countries.

(ii) It is well recognized that cross-border movements of capital, exchange-rate fluctuations and other related features have important implications for the developing countries' production and trade of goods and services. Addressing these will entail policies and measures beyond the remit of the WTO. A set of recommendations in these areas may be worked out and placed before governments and relevant international bodies for consideration.

# Chapter 11

# TRADE AND TRANSFER OF TECHNOLOGY

## FRAMEWORK

THE framework for the WTO's examination of the relationship between trade and transfer of technology is contained in paragraph 37 of the Doha Declaration. It calls for possible recommendations on steps to increase flows of technology to the developing countries. Some discussions have taken place in the WTO working group concerned, but there has not been much progress.

## SUGGESTIONS: WHAT SHOULD BE DONE?

While working out appropriate recommendations, the relevant measures and policies within the framework of the WTO may be identified and given focused attention. For example, some of the aspects within the remit of the WTO that have a direct bearing on the transfer of technology to the developing countries are:

(i) the Agreement on Trade-Related Investment Measures (TRIMs)/Article III of the GATT 1994, which prohibit imposition of the domestic-content requirement which can have a good potential for motivating a producer/investor to build up domestic capacity with higher technology;
(ii) the provision of the Agreement on Subsidies and Countervailing Measures that does not allow subsidies contingent on using domestic products;
(iii) the TRIPS Agreement, which does not stipulate conditions of technology transfer attached to the granting of patents.

Recommendations may include suggesting changes to these agreements so that they contribute positively to the transfer of technology to the developing countries.

# Chapter 12

# OVERALL BALANCE OF INTERESTS: MAKE-OR-BREAK ISSUES

HAVING gone over the different subjects in the current negotiations, it may now be relevant to list out the points of critical importance to the developing countries and the developed countries in the negotiations.

For the major developed countries, the issues of critical interest appear to be: substantial reduction in the developing countries' tariffs on agricultural products, substantial reduction in the developing countries' tariffs on industrial products, and the expansion of the specific commitments of the developing countries in some services sectors.

For the developing countries, the issues of critical interest appear to be: elimination/substantial reduction of agricultural export subsidies and domestic subsidies in the developed countries, substantial reduction of tariffs on some agricultural products, substantial reduction in tariff peaks on industrial products, lessening of constraints on the movement of natural persons for providing services in the developed countries, and tightening of countervailing-duty and anti-dumping-duty processes in the developed countries. Their defensive interests appear to be: protecting domestic agricultural production against heavily subsidized imports from the developed countries and preventing deindustrialization as a result of heavy imports of industrial products.

Of course, all proposals placed by the developed countries and the developing countries should be considered important, but these core issues appear to be critical to the conclusion of the negotiations.

There is therefore a need for a great deal of sensitivity on these separate sets of issues of deep interest to the developed countries and to the developing countries. Instead of repeating the demands and advising others how much they themselves will gain by making concessions, it will be helpful if each tries to understand the interests and compulsions of the other. For example, if two sides have strong compulsions in certain matters and cannot possibly yield their positions, both must work out agreed safeguards against the resulting damages and dangers. In this process, sincerity and sympathy should replace the battle of wits in the negotiations.

For example, if, in the area of agriculture, the developed countries have enormous domestic compulsions not to eliminate their domestic support (of various types, viz., Amber Box, Blue Box and Green Box), they should offer counter-measures in the nature of effective relief to the developing countries. Some such counter-measures may be: a Special Safeguard Mechanism that can be conveniently invoked by the developing countries, and suspension of the implementation of the tariff-reduction obligations of the developing countries until all the domestic support is eliminated.

# Chapter 13

# BUILDING CONFIDENCE

A successful conclusion of the current negotiations depends on building up confidence and credibility in the WTO negotiating process. A crisis of confidence has developed which was amply manifested during the Cancun Ministerial Conference and even in the preparatory process leading to that conference. It is in the interest of the WTO system that this atmosphere of suspicion is replaced by one of amity, trust and mutual understanding. And therein lies the responsibility of all Members, particularly the major developed countries.

Ever since the mid-course of the Uruguay Round and progressively more thereafter, the major developed countries have pressed for accommodation of their interests without being prepared to give anything significant in return. The developing countries were dismayed by these pressures and gradually developed a sense of frustration and helplessness. A feeling is widespread in the developing countries that the WTO process is all about giving in to the demands of the major developed countries without getting any significant concessions in return. This deep frustration of the developing countries was apparent from the statements made by several of their Ministers during and after various Ministerial Conferences.

But the developing countries could not remain content just by expressing their helplessness, frustration and anger. The evolving frame of the WTO was imposing on them added obligations, whether or not they willingly agreed to the various agreements. Their agriculture, industry and trade started feeling the impact of the operation of the WTO agreements. The NGOs in various developing countries began to analyze the issues and build up opinions for defending the interests of their countries and the developing countries in general. Parliamentarians and social groups got alert to the new dangers. All this built up pressures on the governments in the developing countries. The Ministers and senior officers could not just continue with the explanation that they were pressurized into making concessions. Domestic pressures built up on them to resist the pressures in the WTO negotiations.

At the same time, the developing countries started preparing themselves seriously for the negotiations. While they had very much been passive participants at the final stages of decision-making earlier, they came up with nearly 100 proposals in preparation for the Seattle Ministerial Conference. They persisted with these proposals in spite of some efforts to push them off the table. And finally these proposals took formal shape in the form of the implementation issues in the WTO.

The developing countries have continued with their preparations. They have also built up coordination among themselves. As the major developed countries found out in the Cancun Ministerial Conference, they could not just ignore the developing countries and impose their will all the way. The conference collapsed. The major developed countries continued with a sullen attitude for some months thereafter, but they soon realized that they would have to enlist the cooperative support of the developing countries.

A healthy multilateral system is good for all. And it will be healthy if all its members have hopes of deriving shared benefits from it and have confidence that they will get them. This is what is to be built up and the major developed countries have a big role in it. If they become sensitive to the interests and compulsions of the developing countries, the situation will certainly improve.

That is the key to the success of the current negotiations.

# Chapter 14

# AVOIDING TRAPS AND PITFALLS IN THE WTO NEGOTIATIONS

IN view of the widespread and deep implications for the developing countries of the current negotiations in the WTO, it is important for them to guard against traps and pitfalls in the negotiating process. Lessons learnt from the existing WTO agreements should be cause for caution enough. Often there are problems in the language of the agreed texts, in the fine print, in between the lines and in the footnotes and annexes. The developing countries are handicapped by inadequate financial resources and technical expertise. Often they are rushed by the momentum of the WTO process into agreeing to texts to which they did not have the opportunity to devote much attention. An attempt is made here to discuss some of the major types of problems in the negotiating process and the resulting texts.

We should consider all this in the context of the objective of having agreements in the WTO which contain enforceable provisions of rights and obligations. Hence clarity of language in such provisions is essential. Also, it is important to ensure that a short, seemingly innocuous phrase placed somewhere in the text does not detract from the rigour of enforceability of a provision. Such little intrusions in an agreement, whether unintentional or deliberate, will give free play to the dispute settlement panels and Appellate Body to engage in elaborate exercises of "interpretation" through a labyrinth of legal jargon that may be beyond the comprehension, or even test the patience, of negotiators, trade policy officials and the people in trade and industry, particularly of the developing countries. Now that important new agreements are being worked out in the Doha Work Programme negotiations in the WTO, it is necessary to go over what should be included in the texts and what should not.

## SCHEDULE OF NEGOTIATIONS: AVOIDING RUSH

The problem in the negotiations starts with the drawing up and operation of tight negotiating schedules. Often the developing countries' negotiators find themselves totally submerged in the process. They have hardly any time to prepare their proposals or responses to the proposals of others. They are pushed forward by the momentum normally generated by the major developed countries. And in the end they find it practically impossible to make any significant contribution to the negotiations. Agreements are reached without their effective participation. In this manner, obligations are cast on all Members, including the developing countries that had not much time and opportunity to weigh the consequences and put across their points of view effectively. It is necessary for the developing countries to change this trend.

Furthermore, the tight schedules are not always conducive to ensuring a fast pace in the negotiations. When matters of serious obligations affecting a large number of the developing countries are involved, they have a natural tendency to take a defensive position if they are not fully prepared to participate in the negotiations. This often prompts them to say "no", and that blocks the progress of the negotiations. Hence it is also in the wider interest of the WTO system, apart from the interest of the developing countries, to have a reasonable schedule of negotiations and to modulate it on a dynamic basis.

The schedule is initially prepared by the WTO Secretariat, which is naturally interested in encouraging rapid progress in the negotiations. The chairman of the negotiating group concerned then holds consultations and puts the schedule before the group for approval. Normally no one bothers at that time about the future implications and the schedule is approved by the negotiating group. It is only later that the developing countries realize that they have been put under severe pressure of time because of the schedule of formal negotiating meetings. This is further aggravated by a large number of informal meetings and consultations if the subject of the negotiations is a complex one.

As the process of negotiations will result in serious obligations on their governments, the developing countries' negotiators have every right to suggest and insist on modification of the schedule of formal meetings and informal consultations if they cannot cope with it. It is necessary for them to ensure that they have a full grip on the negotiations and are not swept away by the negotiating current. If necessary, they should insist on the postponement of sessions, meetings and decisions. If even 10-15 of them join together in this effort, they can succeed in moulding the pace of negotiations in accordance with their preparedness.

The chairman may like to hurry the process as he may naturally be interested in bringing the negotiations to a quick conclusion. The major developed countries may also like to force the pace of negotiations as it is mostly the subjects of their interest which are in the forefront of the negotiations (with the subjects of interest to the developing countries generally put on the backburner or blocked by technical intricacies, as in the case of the implementation issues, special and differential treatment, and services safeguards in the current negotiations). In this background, the developing countries have to be particularly careful to ensure that the schedule of negotiations is suited to their resources and preparedness.

## INTERIM AGREED TEXT: BASIS FOR NEGOTIATION

The next important stage in the negotiating process comes when a document is prepared which will become the basis for further negotiations. It is an interim document that determines to a great extent the course of further negotiations. It normally lists out the topics of negotiation and may also mention some substantive elements such as the direction of possible rights and obligations. As the issues will not have been resolved at that stage, it may also include some alternative formulations on some subjects.

This interim document forming the basis for further negotiations is important and should be finalized with care. It is necessary for the developing countries to ensure that the topics of their interest as well as the substantive points within each such topic are included in the paper. Special attention from their side is needed, as there has been a tendency in the past few years to leave out their topics and substantive points in these interim texts.

The topics and specific elements of interest to the developing countries must be placed at full parity with those of interest to the developed countries. Keeping them out or assigning them lower parity would weaken the negotiating position of the developing countries right from the start of the substantive negotiations.

Sometimes, a particular course of action in a topic is specified in the interim text which is different from what the developing countries would like to have. It is necessary in these cases to ensure that the course of action of their choice is also included as an alternative that is fully on par with the other option.

It is relevant to recall some recent examples. The then chairmen of the General Council of the WTO prepared texts for consideration by the Ministerial Conferences in Doha in 2001 and in Cancun in 2003. As a large number of developing countries noted on those occasions, these papers contained mostly points of interest to the developed countries and left out the points of interest to the developing countries. The developing countries were thus put to a great disadvantage in these conferences.

Some more recent examples will clarify the problem further. Annex A on agriculture in the July 04 decision contains provisions on the Blue Box subsidies. Paragraph 13 specifies two criteria for the Blue Box, either of which can be applied by a country. Paragraph 14 then says that "the above criteria, along with additional criteria will be negotiated". This latter provision does keep the applicability of the Blue Box an open issue, but the position is still not balanced between the interests of the major developed countries that want to use the Blue Box and the developing countries that oppose it. On the one side, details of criteria have been specified, but on the other side there is no balancing provision. Paragraph 14 does not provide sufficient balance. A proper balance would have been achieved by having a counter-provision saying that the Blue Box would not be continued beyond a particular period. Then these two alternative positions would have been the subject of negotiations. As the situation now stands, however, the developing countries have a handicap in as much as their position is not placed as an alternative at all.

We may take Annex B of the July 04 decision on NAMA as another example. Though paragraph 1 keeps options open by stipulating that there will be additional negotiations to finalize the main elements of the annex, the position is not balanced between the interests of the developed countries and the developing countries. The positions of the developed countries have been elaborately specified in various paragraphs in the annex while there is a total absence of any alternatives based on the positions of the developing countries. For example, paragraph 4 says: "... the (NAMA) Negotiating Group should continue its work on a non-linear formula applied on a line-by-line basis ..." Then paragraph 8 specifies that some percentage of the tariff lines will be subjected to less than formula cuts. Here the direction of obligation is broadly in line with the positions of the developed countries. The developing countries do not want a non-linear formula to be applied to them, nor do they want line-by-line cuts; they do not want to go beyond a percentage cut of their average tariffs. Their position is not reflected at all in the text.

Annex B is very much imbalanced as it totally leaves out the positions of the developing countries. A balance could have been achieved by including formulations on cutting average tariffs by a simple percentage as alternatives to paragraphs 4 and 8. Now, however, the developing countries will be starting from a handicap, since the positions of the developed countries have already found a place in the text (though subject to further negotiations) while the positions of the developing countries are totally absent.

Using such an imbalanced paper to form the basis of negotiations stacks the deck against the developing countries. This imbalance costs them considerable negotiating leverage right from the beginning of the negotiations on substantive matters of rights and obligations.

A balance can also be ensured by leaving out altogether the opposing positions of the developed countries and developing countries and including provisions which could be considered to be somewhere in between the two. This would not put any one side to a disadvantage and both sides would negotiate from the middle position.

In summary, it is important for the developing countries to pay as much attention to the interim text that forms the basis for negotiations as to the final text that prescribes the rights and obligations. The developing countries should get their topics and specific elements within the individual topics included in this interim text. It will be fully rational for them to refuse to take an interim paper as the basis for further negotiations if the paper has ignored their topics and their elements within individual topics while including those of the developed countries.

## FINAL AGREED TEXT

### *PREAMBLE AND EXPRESSION OF INTENTIONS*

Let us now take up the issue of the final negotiated text. It must be noted that emphatic words in the preamble of the agreement or noble intentions strongly expressed in various articles of the text may not actually amount to a specification of any rights and obligations. Their utility lies only in cases where some vague language in a provision of the agreement needs to be interpreted. If the language of an article in the agreement is patently clear on the rights and obligations, the preamble or other statements in the agreement are not consulted while interpreting the agreement.

Nevertheless, these parts of an agreement are not totally useless or unnecessary. They have considerable political significance in that they indicate the agreed principles, objectives and aims behind the agreement to which the countries will be considered bound. They help point to the general trend of thinking in the area covered by the agreement and the shared priorities of the countries. Accordingly they contribute to the interpretation of a provision when the language of that provision is not clear. Also, when an amendment to the agreement is proposed, it can be supported or opposed on the basis of whether or not it is in consonance with the preamble.

However, a clear provision on rights and obligations remains operative even if it is somewhat inconsistent with the preamble or other general statements in various parts of the agreement. The following are some examples of the inefficacy of the preamble and expressions of intentions.

The first sentence of the Marrakesh Agreement Establishing the WTO includes as an objective: "… ensuring full employment and a large and steadily growing volume of real income and effective demand, and expanding the production of and trade in goods and services …" This is among the parameters within which the WTO agreements have been placed. However, several measures taken under various agreements operate directly against this objective. For example, when restrictive measures are taken under authorization by the Agreements on Subsidies and Countervailing Measures, Anti-dumping and Safeguards, they do not contribute to ensuring full employment and growing real income or expansion of production and trade in goods and services, yet those actions are not illegal as they are authorized by specific provisions of the agreements.

Article 15 of the Agreement on Anti-dumping says: "It is recognized that special regard must be given by developed country Members to the special situation of developing country Members when considering the application of anti-dumping measures under this Agreement". This recognition nevertheless does not make the anti-dumping actions of the developed countries against the developing countries illegal if they have followed the procedures prescribed in the Anti-dumping

Agreement. It has not even discouraged them from taking actions against the developing countries; in fact, most of their actions are against the developing countries.

Article 27.1 of the Agreement on Subsidies and Countervailing Measures recognizes that subsidies may play an important role in economic development programmes of developing countries. However, this has not been translated into specific rights for developing countries.

Article IV of the GATS has elaborate coverage of the intention to facilitate the increasing participation of the developing countries in world trade in services. But the operative parts of the agreement on rights and obligations are in effect aimed at improving the market access of the services of the *developed* countries in the developing countries. There is nothing special in these provisions that would facilitate the developing countries' production and export of services. Still, none of these provisions have ever been constrained in their operation by this expression of intention in Article IV.

Article 7 of the TRIPS Agreement includes among the agreement's objectives: "The protection and enforcement of intellectual property rights should contribute ... to the transfer and dissemination of technology, to the mutual advantage of producers and users of technological knowledge ..." In spite of this pious intention, clearly defined obligations in the agreement never get tested as to whether the measures taken in accordance with them actually contribute to the transfer of technology or whether they are to the mutual advantage of producers and users of the technology. In fact, nearly all of the clearly defined provisions in the agreement are about ensuring protection of the rights of the producers of technology. Exceptions to these rights aimed at safeguarding the users' interests are provided for only sparingly in some provisions, and that too with much less specificity and ease of invocation.

The Arrangement Regarding International Trade in Textiles (commonly known as the Multi-fibre Agreement, MFA) has a provision in Article 6.1 which recognizes the need to provide more favourable terms to the imports from developing countries in applying restrictions. However, this did not prevent or dissuade the developed countries from applying trade restrictions exclusively against the developing countries. Nor were their actions declared illegal if they had followed the procedures provided in the agreement.

There are many other such examples which show that, though important, the general provisions of an agreement do not add to or subtract from the rights and obligations. To that extent, they are not of much practical use. The developing countries may, of course, pay attention to them in the final text to ensure that they include their version of the objectives and aims. But it is not worthwhile to spend a lot of time on them. A preferred course may be to have one simple sentence in the preamble or not to have any preamble at all. That will save the developing countries' negotiators some energy which can then be applied to examining the operative parts of the agreement.

## *LANGUAGE OF COMPULSORY OBLIGATIONS*

A provision with "shall" or "must" usually makes the subsequent part of the sentence a mandatory obligation. A provision with "should" does not make the requirement obligatory; it will be treated only as a form of guidance. Some examples below will clarify this distinction.

Article XVI.4 of the Marrakesh Agreement Establishing the WTO says: "Each Member shall ensure the conformity of its laws, regulations and administrative procedures with its obligations as provided in the annexed Agreements". "Shall ensure" here makes the obligation of conformity absolute and unqualified.

Article 5.4 of the Agreement on the Application of Sanitary and Phytosanitary Measures provides: "Members should, when determining the appropriate level of sanitary or phytosanitary protection, take into account the objective of minimizing negative trade effects". Here, the use of "should" (instead of "shall") means the requirement is only a guidance and not an enforceable obligation.

## *DILUTED "COMPULSIONS"*

The compulsory obligation which comes with "shall" can nevertheless be made ineffective by adding stipulations like "shall endeavour to", "shall as far as possible", "shall as far as practicable", "shall aim at", etc. These phrases do not make the obligation enforceable. The country that is asked to "endeavour to" comply with some condition can simply ignore it; its failure to comply with that provision cannot be challenged in the dispute settlement process of the WTO. An example is given below.

Article 15 of the Anti-dumping Agreement specifies that "possibilities of constructive remedies … shall be explored before applying anti-dumping duties". The binding obligation that may otherwise have arisen from "shall" has been diluted twice over by the use of "possibilities" and "explored". In fact, certain dispute settlement panels have been of the view that this provision does not even require a country to provide or accept any constructive remedy that may be identified or offered. Further, a country may start the "exploration" and simply conclude that no possibilities exist.

Such provisions should not satisfy the countries in whose ostensible interest these conditions or measures have been included in the text.

## *INEFFECTIVE "COMPULSIONS"*

Sometimes, the language in an agreement appears clear and of a compulsory nature, and yet the rights and obligations it supposedly entails cannot be utilized. It is thus ineffective and almost useless. An important example is Article XIX.2 of the GATS that says: "There shall be appropriate flexibility for individual developing country Members for opening fewer sectors, liberalizing fewer types of transactions

..." The way this particular right of the developing countries has been expressed here does not make it enforceable. "Shall" in this provision does have the appearance of being strong and mandatory as it normally is, but it is not clear on whom the obligation falls and in what way it will be implemented.

This provision relates to specific sectoral obligations on liberalization of services trade. The process of negotiations for this purpose involves a series of bilateral negotiations between the countries for mutual give-and-take in various services sectors. This is a confidential process and the results of the bilateral negotiations are made public only after the conclusion of all such negotiations. While the bilateral negotiations between a developing country and a developed country are going on, the former can, of course, quote this provision of "mandatory" flexibility, but the latter may just ignore it and insist instead on *higher* levels of liberalization by the developing country, as indeed was the case during the negotiations for liberalization of financial services. No mechanism is prescribed or specified here that can make this provision binding on the developed country engaged in negotiations on specific sectoral obligations with a developing country.

The weakness in the formulation of this right of the developing countries, therefore, is that it does not specify on whom the obligation falls and how it will be enforced in practice.

It is necessary to ensure that the language of an obligation clearly specifies on whom the obligation lies. The utility of a right should be tested by exploring answers to questions like "On whom does the obligation fall?" and "If my country is denied this right, in what manner will my country enforce it? Will my country be able to take recourse to the Dispute Settlement Understanding in the WTO against those who are denying it this right?"

## *VAGUE PROVISIONS*

Sometimes there are some vague provisions in the agreements that create many problems in implementation. Some examples are given below.

Article 9.1 of the Agreement on Safeguards provides that safeguard measures shall not be applied against a product originating in a developing country "as long as" its share of imports of the product concerned in the importing country does not exceed 3 percent. A question has arisen as to whether this *de minimis* requirement applies only during the period of investigation or also subsequent to the application of the safeguard measure. One possibility is that the imports from a developing country, in order to qualify for exemption, would be required to remain below the *de minimis* level even after the safeguard measure comes into force. In that case, if the imports exceed the *de minimis* level, the next question is whether a fresh review is necessary to include the developing country concerned in the application of the safeguard measure.

Another example is Articles 4.10/4.11 of the Agreement on Subsidies and Countervailing Measures. These provide for appropriate countermeasures against prohibited subsidies. Footnotes 9/10 specify that "this expression is not meant to allow countermeasures that are disproportionate in light of the fact that the subsidies dealt with under these provisions are prohibited". This has been found to be an extremely vague provision. The dispute settlement panels considering these footnotes have not been able to discern their meaning clearly.

Sometimes, a provision in an agreement is deliberately kept vague. One reason may be that the participants in the negotiations that drew up the agreement wanted to keep a range of options open and allow flexibility to the countries to adopt any of those options. Another reason may be that the participants could not come to an agreement on the specificity of this provision and left it in a vague form as agreement on other important issues had been reached and they did not want to hold up the final agreement just for this one provision.

In the former case, it would have been better to specify the permissible options; otherwise the dispute settlement panels and Appellate Body will take upon themselves the responsibility of interpreting the vague provision and their interpretation may not go exactly in the same direction as the participants had wanted. In any case, retaining a vague provision gives occasion for raising disputes in the future. Hence it is much better to mention the options clearly if options are to be allowed.

But if the latter is the case, one cannot help the matter going into the hands of the panels and Appellate Body.

## *"SAFE HAVENS": CIRCUMVENTING OBLIGATIONS*

Sometimes, serious obligations are avoided or bypassed by the inclusion of some provisions elsewhere in the agreement. These are the "safe havens" for escaping from obligations. Some well-known examples are given below.

The Agreement on Textiles and Clothing made it obligatory for the major developed countries to undertake progressive liberalization in this sector by bringing some products into the fold of the normal GATT/WTO rules (they had previously been under the special restrictive regime of the MFA). The liberalization was to be effected in four instalments, such that only products covering 49 percent of imports were to be still left out of the liberalization process by the end of 2002. And there was to be full coverage of liberalization by the end of 2004.

The major developed countries fulfilled their obligation of progressively liberalizing the stipulated percentages of textiles and clothing imports without, however, actually bringing about any effective liberalization during the transition period. This was made possible by using a loophole in the agreement. The agreement included an annex containing the list of products which would form the base for calculating the percentages to be progressively liberalized. The major developed countries adopted the clever device of selecting products from this annex that were not under restraint and, in fact, were never under restraint. They "liberalized" these products at various stages of the implementation process and thereby fulfilled their obligation as far as the percentages were concerned. But they substantially left out the products that were or had been under restraint. Thus the developing exporting countries could not derive the expected benefit from the implementation of the agreement.

This "safe haven" was created by the major developed countries by first putting a long list of products in the annex, even though some of these products had never been under restraint or had no possibility of being under any restraint in the near future. Then they principally selected from the annex such products that had not been under restraint anyway to be "liberalized".

With hindsight, we now see that this pitfall could have been avoided in two ways: either by including in the annex only products that were relevant for the liberalization process (i.e., only those that were under restraint or had been under restraint in the past) or by clearly stipulating that a certain percentage of the selected products at each stage of liberalization had to be made up of those that were under restraint at that time or in the past. This clarity could have closed off the escape route.

Another example of a safe haven can be found in the Agreement on Agriculture. Under this agreement, the obligation was that countries would reduce their domestic agricultural subsidies by stipulated percentages every year to achieve a certain percentage of reduction by the end of the implementation period. The major developed countries carried out this obligation in accordance with the agreement, but, to the dismay of the developing countries, the domestic subsidies actually *increased*. This was made possible through an escape route which had been carefully put in the agreement. The agreement recognized two types of domestic subsidies that were not subjected to the obligation of reduction. These were: subsidies under Article 6.5 (Blue Box subsidies) and under Annex 2 (Green Box subsidies). The major developed countries fulfilled their obligation of reducing the reducible subsidies but, at the same time, increased the other subsidies that were not subject to the reduction obligation and thus managed to increase their total subsidies.

Again, hindsight indicates that the loophole could have been closed by either not having any non-reducible category of subsidies or stipulating that the non-reducible subsidies could not be raised.

Also, the "sunset" clause (Article 11.3) of the Agreement on Anti-dumping has a built-in safe-haven provision. It says: "… any definitive anti-dumping duty shall be terminated on a date not later than five years from its imposition … unless the authorities determine, in a review before that date ..., that the expiry of the duty would be likely to lead to continuation or recurrence of dumping and injury. The duty may remain in force pending the outcome of such a review". The first part of this provision is strong and one expects that the duty will really be terminated at the end of five years. But the second part makes this compulsion extremely soft. A country can go about the review and conveniently come to the conclusion that termination of the duty would result in a recurrence of dumping and injury. In fact, in the case of some major developed countries, the process of this review is such that the duty has continued well beyond the five-year period.

Another iniquitous safe haven for the developed countries is to be found in the proviso to item (k) in Annex I to the Agreement on Subsidies and Countervailing Measures. Under this proviso, export credits given in accordance with the OECD credit arrangements will not be considered to be export subsidies. This is a carve-out of a safe haven for the developed countries against the prohibition of export credits. Moreover, there is a further expansion of the safe haven. In case the OECD arrangements are modified in future and come to enhance the coverage of export credits, this proviso will continue to apply to the enhanced export credits as well.

## *UNCLEAR PROVISIONS: POTENTIAL DANGERS*

It is important that a provision not be included in an agreement if its meaning or implication is not clear. Sometimes, such provisions enter innocuously only to create tremendous problems later. Examples thereof are Article 6.5 and Annex 2 of the Agriculture Agreement. When they found entry into the text, the developing countries did not really know what they meant or involved. It was thought to be some minor enabling provision for meeting certain eventualities. But they turned out to be veritable highways for escape routes, as explained above.

In retrospect, it appears desirable that the developing countries should have sought clarification from the US and EU about how such provisions were to be applied in practice by them and what the amounts involved in these subsidies were. If the full details had been available at the time these provisions were worked out, it is likely that the developing countries would have hesitated in agreeing to them. In fact, even some academic experts did not fully grasp the implications. They made projections of the expected rise in agriculture trade without taking into account these heavy subsidies that were to continue and even be increased. Most of the projections for the agriculture sector did not materialize as these unclear elements had not been accounted for.

Given these lessons to be drawn from past experience, utmost care should now be taken so that only clearly understood provisions are placed in an agreement. One should not feel embarrassed in seeking clarifications from the proponents of a provision until the meaning or implication is totally clear. After all, the agreements impose serious obligations; hence the negotiators of developing countries should not hesitate to ensure they are fully satisfied about the implications before they agree to a provision in an agreement.

## *ANNEXES AND FOOTNOTES*

The annexes and footnotes in the WTO agreements are important. Very often they are not just clarificatory provisions; instead, they contain substantive elements of rights and obligations. For example, footnote 9 of the Agreement on Anti-dumping and footnote 45 of the Agreement on Subsidies and Countervailing Measures define the scope of "injury", which is an important element in deciding on an anti-dumping duty or countervailing duty, and footnote 1 in the Dispute Settlement Understanding defines "decision by consensus", which is an important part of the decision-making process in the WTO. The importance of some annexes of the Agreement on Agriculture and Agreement on Textiles and Clothing was discussed earlier. Annexes I, II and III of the Agreement on Subsidies and Countervailing Measures give provisions for a list of export subsidies and for calculation of the subsidy margin in domestic subsidies. These are all very substantive provisions. Furthermore, there are a large number of footnotes: the Agreement on Subsidies and Countervailing Measures has 68 of them and the Agreement on Anti-dumping has 24.

Considering the importance of footnotes and annexes, the developing countries should not let them pass as mere explanatory or clarificatory notes; they should examine them minutely with the same attention as devoted to substantive articles of the agreements.

## EVALUATION OF RESULTS

After an agreement is reached in the negotiations, the authorities in the developing countries should evaluate the results carefully before accepting it and ratifying it. Following the strains of intense negotiations, there may be a tendency to draw some relief and satisfaction from having made the developed countries climb down from their extreme initial positions. The negotiators may also succumb to the error of projecting the result as a gain if they have succeeded in diluting these extreme initial positions. But this is not a correct way to evaluate the results.

The benchmark for evaluation should not be the initial position of the other side. The appropriate benchmark should be the rights and obligations existing before the agreement. The evaluation of gain and loss should be made with reference to this benchmark. Consequently, the criterion for a qualitative evaluation of gain or loss should not be how far the other side has climbed down from its initial position. The real criterion should be the shift in the rights and obligations. A country should examine the extent of rights it has given up for the benefit of others and the rights the others have given up and from which it will benefit. It is on such an assessment that it should finally decide whether to agree to the final text.

# Chapter 15

# DIFFICULT PATH AHEAD IN THE WTO

## EARLY CONCESSIONS BY DEVELOPING COUNTRIES

### *BACKGROUND*

INTENSE negotiations continued after the adoption of the July 04 decision, but no agreement emerged on the main issues. Consequently the Hong Kong Ministerial Conference of the WTO in December 2005 came up with only a meagre outcome. No significant progress could be made even subsequently. The negotiations collapsed and were then suspended during the last week of July 2006.

In the process of these negotiations, the developing countries made several significant concessions without getting any commensurate benefits. They gave up some of their important options, particularly in the areas of agriculture, NAMA and services. There was no compulsion on them to do so, nor was there any incentive for them to take this initiative. Perhaps they wanted to demonstrate their spirit of cooperation in the multilateral negotiations by coming forward with some important concessions. It is to be watched whether the developed countries will respond positively to their constructive gesture. Past experiences have shown, however, that the developed countries mostly consider such early concessions from the developing countries as a sign of weakness and are encouraged to raise their expectations and demands. Some of the important early concessions made by the developing countries are described below.

### *INDUSTRIAL TARIFFS (NAMA)*

*(i)* *Argentina-Brazil-India proposal*: Argentina, Brazil and India jointly put forward a proposal in April 2005 that tariff reduction should be on the basis of the Swiss formula with a coefficient that would be dependent on the average tariff of a country. This was a major concession as it implied that they had accepted reduction of *each* bound tariff. Never in the past had the developing countries undertaken an obligation of reducing industrial tariffs on a line-by-line (of each product individually) basis. Earlier their obligation had been limited to reducing the average tariff; they retained the option to 'spread' the reduced average over the entire range of products. This had allowed them the

flexibility to modulate individual tariffs in accordance with their development interests. Now by giving this proposal, Argentina, Brazil and India have surrendered this vital flexibility. Perhaps they expected a positive result of having to undertake lower tariff reduction through a higher coefficient in the formula, based on their rather high average tariffs.

*(ii)* *Hong Kong decision on tariff reduction:* The adverse aspect of this proposal was given a seal of approval in the Hong Kong Ministerial Declaration, while the expected positive aspect did not materialize. It was decided to adopt the Swiss formula for tariff reduction and the choice of coefficients was left open. Thus the developing countries lost their flexibility of selecting the products for high/low rates of reduction without obtaining the expected benefit of lower reduction.

*(iii)* *Hong Kong decision on tariff binding:* On the binding coverage of tariffs (the percentage of tariff lines covered by a tariff-binding commitment), the decision in Hong Kong was that in the case of currently unbound tariffs, there would be a mark-up from the currently applied rates and then reduction would be effected according to the Swiss formula. The implication is that all products will be covered by the binding commitment. This also is a big concession made by the developing countries. Currently the developed countries have nearly total binding coverage, while the developing countries have a much lower binding coverage. And all this is a part of the current rights and obligations of the countries in the GATT/WTO system. With the Hong Kong decision implying full binding coverage, the developing countries have given up their right of keeping some of their products out of the commitment of binding. In this way another significant flexibility has been surrendered.

## *AGRICULTURE*

The Hong Kong Ministerial Declaration has decided that the export subsidies in agriculture will be eliminated by the end of 2013. On the face of it, this may appear to be a gain for the developing countries, as they have been demanding the elimination of these subsidies. But a closer look indicates that even this decision entails a major concession by the developing countries.

The decision implies that the export subsidies will continue in the major developed countries until 2013. This is a big tragedy. Export subsidies are provided mainly by the major developed countries, particularly the EU and the US, the former by means of direct payments and the latter in the form of export credits and food aid. It puts the farmers of the importing countries at a great disadvantage and, in the case of the developing countries, even threatens their income and livelihood. There is absolutely no justification for these subsidies to continue even for a day longer. Now the Hong Kong decision ensures their continuance until 2013.

## *SERVICES*

A close look at the decision on services in the Hong Kong Ministerial Declaration will reveal some subtle but significant concessions by the developing countries. It has been decided to intensify negotiations in accordance with the objectives and approaches contained in Annex C to the Declaration. This annex says that commitments will be taken at existing levels of market access in Mode 1 (supply of service by the service provider of a country to a consumer located in another country) and Mode 2 (supply of service in a country to a consumer coming from another country). In respect of Mode 3 (supply of service through the commercial presence of a foreign firm), the annex asks for commitments on enhanced levels of foreign equity participation and elimination or substantial reduction of necessity criteria applied by a country.

These are major commitments in view of the current flexibility available to the developing countries in the GATS. The GATS permits the countries to choose the services sectors to be liberalized and also to impose conditions and limitations on market access and national treatment in these sectors. In particular, the agreement stipulates that the developing countries shall have the flexibility to liberalize fewer sectors and fewer transactions. But the decision in Hong Kong mentioned above lays down the base level for liberalization across the board in all sectors. The developing countries have given up their options and flexibility to a significant extent by agreeing to this decision.

## *DECISIONS FAVOURABLE TO DEVELOPING COUNTRIES*

The Hong Kong Ministerial Declaration has two decisions in the area of agriculture that are favourable to the developing countries: (i) these countries can self-designate some products as Special Products; and (ii) those developing countries that do not have the obligation to reduce their Amber Box subsidies can retain their permissible *de minimis* level of domestic subsidies. Such clarity about the selection of Special Products is a step forward, but its practical utility is uncertain, as the number of products to be so designated and the special treatment to be given to them are still undetermined. Similarly retention of the *de minimis* subsidies of the developing countries is also a positive step, but it was never under serious challenge. Perhaps the major developed countries had proposed the reduction of these subsidies more for strategic reasons in order to put the developing countries on the defensive. In any case, this enabling provision is of little use to the developing countries as they do not have adequate financial resources to pay subsidies to their farmers up to this level.

It would thus appear that the Hong Kong Ministerial Declaration is highly unbalanced from the point of view of the developing countries. Their gains have been meagre while they have made major concessions.

## POST-HONG KONG DEVELOPMENTS

The post-Hong Kong phase of negotiations was characterized by artificial dynamism. An atmosphere of crisis and tension was created by having frequent meetings among small groups of trade ministers of WTO Member states at short intervals and fixing unreal targets. Perhaps the strategy was to push the ministers into softening their positions hurriedly. But the stakes and interests were too complex and diverse for such tactics to be effective.

Negotiations were conducted in restrictive and non-transparent formats. Perhaps the aim was to have agreement within a small group of rather active and vocal countries and then expand the circle of acceptance. The earlier negotiating format of "mini-ministerial meetings", which was already very restrictive, was replaced by a still more restrictive and non-transparent format. The trade ministers of Australia, Brazil, Japan, India and the US and the trade commissioner of the European Commission, representing the EU (jointly called "the G6" in WTO parlance), assumed the role of prime movers. They started intense talks among themselves to find common ground. The vast majority of the membership of the WTO that were left out in this process got disturbed and expressed their concern from time to time.

The G6 could not come to an agreement. Their talks collapsed in the last week of July 2006 and they decided to suspend their joint deliberations. The Director-General of the WTO then decided to suspend the negotiating process altogether and informed the WTO Trade Negotiations Committee and the General Council about the suspension. Neither a formal approval of the suspension was sought from the General Council nor was any such approval given by it. The General Council simply took note of the statement of the Director-General. Thus while the WTO Members accepted the suspension, they did not give their seal of approval.

## RESUMPTION OF TALKS LIKELY

There are several shades of opinion on the possibility of the negotiations being restarted. Many experts feel that it is difficult now to restart the process and complete it by the end of June 2007 to catch the deadline of the "fast-track authority" given by the US Congress to the US executive. (The "fast-track authority", technically known as the Trade Promotion Authority, enables the US President to submit a trade agreement to the US Congress for acceptance or rejection in its entirety without any scope for changes and amendments which could hold up the process. This authority will expire at the end of June 2007.) Thus many of them consider the Doha Work Programme negotiations almost dead.

But there are reasonable grounds to anticipate that the negotiations may restart soon and get wound up by end-June 2007. It is reasonable to believe that the manufacturers, exporters and service providers of the major developed countries will expect their governments to consolidate the gains already obtained in these negotiations and several others that seem to be within their reach. All these will be lost if the negotiations do not conclude by the deadline of end-June 2007.

Developing countries' commitments of total binding coverage of industrial tariffs and reduction of tariffs on each industrial product have already been obtained, as explained in the beginning of this chapter. An industrial-tariff ceiling of 20 percent (resulting from a coefficient of 20 in the Swiss formula) and 35-45 percent reduction in the agricultural tariffs in the developing countries appear to be within reach. Besides, significant liberalization in several services sectors through sectoral plurilateral negotiations also appears attainable. The industry, trade and services lobbies in the major developed countries may not like to lose these opportunities for enhanced market access in the developing countries.

The time limit of the "fast-track authority" given by the US Congress may be another motivating factor for expediting the conclusion of the WTO negotiations. If the opportunity is missed now, it may not come again for several years. The shift in the political spectrum in the US Congress is such that many experts think it unlikely that the US executive will get another term of the "fast-track authority". The trade and industry sectors in the US may perhaps expect the new dynamics in the US Congress to look after their sustained defensive interests in the future, but completion of the current negotiations is important for their aggressive export interests. And, it may be possible, under extreme pressure of time, to catch the deadline of end-June 2007 if the negotiations are not delayed too long.

## EMERGING TRENDS IN NEGOTIATIONS

### *SITUATION WITHIN THE G6*

Differences in positions among the G6 countries were really not so wide as to have caused the much-publicized collapse of the negotiations at the end of July 2006. Perhaps the collapse was more due to the timing and the tension in the atmosphere. It is important to understand the positions within the G6 at that terminal phase, as these will have a significant bearing on the negotiations when they resume.

The G6 are reported to have taken up three core issues for resolution: agriculture tariffs in the EU, domestic subsidies in agriculture in the US, and industrial tariffs in the developing countries. The first issue did not prove to be a stumbling block as the EU is reported to have indicated some flexibility. The other two were, however, more difficult.

The G20 developing-country grouping had asked for 70-80 percent reduction in the total trade-distorting domestic support (TDS) in the developed countries. With the levels in the US and EU of US$48 billion and €110 billion (year 2000, the last year of notification) respectively, the G20's expectations of the reduced values were respectively US$12 billion and €27 billion (i.e., after reduction by 70-80 percent). On their part, the US and EU are reported to have offered to reduce the levels to US$23 billion and €33 billion. Perhaps there was some indication that the EU might be finally willing to go down to the level suggested by the G20. Thus the main problem was the refusal of the US to reduce any further.

In respect of industrial tariffs, Brazil and India (members of a coalition of 11 developing countries commonly called NAMA-11) perhaps appeared to be moving towards a coefficient of 25 in the Swiss formula, but the demand from the developed countries was for 15.

These differences were really not totally unbridgeable. For example, there was scope for the US to come down slightly lower in its TDS, say to US$19 billion, which was its applied level in 2005. The freedom to raise the Green Box subsidies and thereby neutralize the effect of any reduction in the TDS could have tempered its hesitation. Similarly, in view of the trends in the negotiating positions of Brazil and India, going slightly lower in the coefficient in the Swiss formula in NAMA was perhaps not totally unlikely.

What the developing countries have to seriously consider is whether these positions, if they had finally emerged, as was likely if the negotiations had continued in a more conducive atmosphere, would be in their interest. As is indicated below, such a result would have been highly dangerous and grossly unfair for the developing countries.

## *DANGERS FOR DEVELOPING COUNTRIES*

### *Agriculture*

Even if the EU and the US would have finally agreed to reduce their respective TDS to the levels of €27 billion and US$19 billion, it would not have defended the farmers of the developing countries against heavily subsidized imports from the EU and the US, nor would it have significantly facilitated their exports to third-country markets. The sad fact is that even if the proposal of the G20 on TDS reduction is fully accepted, it will not effectively protect domestic agricultural production in the developing countries and promote their agricultural exports. This is because of two loopholes and escape routes which may allow the major developed countries to maintain or even increase their total domestic subsidies. These loopholes and escape routes are: (i) Green Box subsidies; and (ii) product concentration of TDS, as will be explained below.

Of course, the G20 has given proposals regarding the Green Box and product concentration too, but these are much less specific than those for the TDS and tariffs. Also, these have not been pursued with the same vigour as that applied to TDS and tariffs. In agriculture, the negotiations in the G6 were allowed to be narrowed down to the issues of tariffs and TDS without simultaneously keeping the criteria for the Green Box and the product ceiling of TDS in the forefront. Relegating these two issues to the background is risky.

The Green Box subsidies are not subject to reduction on the presumption that they are not trade-distorting. But enough evidence is now available to indicate that even such subsidies can distort production and trade. They have a wealth effect and also increase the risk-taking tendency of the farmers. They enhance the staying capacity of the farmers in agriculture and support their otherwise unviable agricultural production.

Some forms of subsidy in the Green Box cause particularly serious concern, for example, decoupled income support, insurance against income loss and investment aid, given respectively under paragraphs 6, 7 and 11 of Annex 2 to the AoA. Any amount can be given through these routes without limit, resulting in limitless distortion of production and thereby of trade. These open and unhindered routes through the Green Box have been variously used by the US and the EU from year to year. For example, the amount of decoupled income support in the US was US$4 billion in 2001 and that of investment aid in the EU was US$5.7 billion in 2001-2.

After reducing their total TDS to an agreed level, the US and EU can easily enhance the amount given under these provisions of the Green Box, thus nullifying the effect of the TDS reduction. All they have to do is to make the relevant changes in their legislation, which would be entirely an internal process. Thus, obtaining a commitment for reduction of the total TDS of the major developed countries without simultaneously and effectively closing the escape route offered by the Green Box may be a fruitless exercise.

The developing countries have the bitter experience of the Uruguay Round, where the major developed countries utilized the escape routes in agriculture and textiles. The developed countries fulfilled their commitment of reducing their Amber Box subsidies, but enhanced their total subsidies in agriculture. In textiles, they fulfilled their obligation of liberalization in four phases without however actually bringing about any effective liberalization for 10 years, from 1995 to 2004. They were able to do these by using the escape routes that had found their way into the respective agreements.

There is no assurance that they will not do the same once again. An effective safeguard can be achieved only by disciplining the criteria of the Green Box, which is already mandated by the July 04 decision.

Another risk arises due to the possibility of concentration of the TDS on a limited number of products. The total TDS in the US and EU, even at reduced levels, can be highly injurious to the developing countries if they are concentrated on a small number of products. In the absence of an effective discipline on the product concentration of the TDS, the major developed countries can select some products to be accorded a very large proportion of the permissible TDS, thus infusing high levels of artificial competitive strength into the selected products.

## *NAMA*

The Hong Kong Ministerial Declaration has decided to use the Swiss formula for tariff reduction in industrial products. This formula links the initial tariff and the final tariff through a coefficient (a number) which is to be determined through negotiation. The choice of the coefficient in this formula is crucial in determining the extent of tariff reduction. The higher the coefficient, the lesser is the extent of reduction. The negotiations have thus been focussed on what the coefficient should be.

The figures under consideration within the G6 reportedly were a coefficient of 20-30 for the developing countries and around 10 for the developed countries. Perhaps this was considered as reflecting the "less than full reciprocity" feature for the developing countries. But a simple calculation would indicate that such an assumption is highly erroneous. Taking 30 as the coefficient for the developing countries, for example, their tariff of 28 percent, which is their average tariff, will be reduced to 14 percent, which represents a 50 percent reduction (from 28 to 14). Taking a coefficient of 10 for the developed countries, their tariff of 4 percent, which is their average tariff, will be reduced to 3 percent, or a reduction of only 25 percent (from 4 to 3). This is clearly a reversal of the agreed principle of "less than full reciprocity" for the developing countries and will be extremely unfair.

## *Services*

As explained earlier, the developing countries have made significant concessions regarding commitments in Modes 1, 2 and 3 in the Hong Kong Ministerial Declaration, detracting from the special and differential treatment allowed to them in Article XIX of the GATS. Moreover, these concessions have not been reciprocated by the developed countries. This is grossly unfair. Reportedly, the G6 did not take up the subject of services in their discussions and thus did not correct this unbalanced and unfair position.

Besides, the plurilateral track of negotiations has assumed a major role where a specific sector or mode will be separately negotiated. There may be a risk that the developing countries will be pressurized to make concessions in specific sectors and modes of interest to the major developed countries, while they lose out in the sectors and modes of interest to themselves. The plurilateral track does not facilitate exchange of concessions across sectors and modes, and this may work against the interests of the developing countries, if enough precaution establishing linkages among different plurilateral tracks is not taken.

## *Subjects Sponsored by the Developing Countries*

The G6 did not take on board the subjects which had been sponsored by the developing countries in the negotiations and which are of special importance to them. These subjects, which have special bearing on the development content of the current negotiations, are: special and differential treatment of the developing countries, implementation issues and non-tariff barriers. These important subjects have been pushed into the background by various means.

The discussion above therefore indicates that the developing countries are exposed to grave risks in the negotiations and it is necessary to reorient the negotiations when they resume in future.

## SOME SUGGESTIONS

### *AGRICULTURE*

#### *Trade-Distorting Domestic Support (TDS)*

There should be the following disciplines on the TDS:

(i) The total TDS, excluding a small *de minimis* amount, in the developed countries should be eliminated by the end of the implementation period.
(ii) Elimination of the TDS should be front-loaded; thus 50 percent of the TDS, excluding a small *de minimis* amount, should be eliminated in the first year of the implementation period.
(iii) The corporate sector should be totally excluded from the benefit of TDS, which should be admissible only to individual farmers.
(iv) There should be an annual ceiling on the payment of TDS to an individual farmer.

#### *Product-Specific Ceiling of TDS*

There should be a ceiling on the TDS given to a product. As some selected products have been getting high subsidies in the major developed countries in the past, it will not be correct to base the ceiling on the level in a previous year. The ceiling should instead be fixed as a percentage of annual production, for example, the subsidy on any product may not be allowed to exceed 10 percent of its annual production.

#### *Green Box Subsidies*

The Doha Declaration and the July 04 decision have already mandated a review of the criteria for the Green Box subsidies to ensure they are not trade-distorting or cause only minimal trade distortion. As mentioned earlier, Green Box subsidies, by enhancing the staying capacity of the farmer in farming and thus supporting otherwise unviable production, are very much trade-distorting. An effective way to stop Green

Box subsidies from being trade-distorting is, of course, to prohibit these payments altogether. If that is not possible, these payments should be kept at a minimal level in order to minimize the trade distortion.

The Green Box subsidies, particularly those handed out as decoupled income support, insurance against income loss and investment aid, given respectively under paragraphs 6, 7 and 11 of Annex 2 to the AoA, should be subjected to specific criteria of eligibility and a ceiling. Suggestions for some criteria are given below:

(i) Payment should be made only to individual farmers. Corporate entities should be totally excluded from such payment.

(ii) Even among the individual farmers, there should be some criterion of eligibility based on income, in recognition of the fact that comparatively richer farmers do not need this support. For example, only the farmers having an annual income from all sources of up to 10 percent of the average annual income in the country may be made eligible for the payment.

(iii) There should be a ceiling on the annual payment to an individual farmer, for example, US$5,000 to 10,000.

### *Quantitative Restrictions*

Developing countries should be enabled to impose quantitative import restrictions on the products that have received TDS or Green Box subsidies of the types mentioned above.

### *Other Important Elements*

Apart from the subsidy-specific suggestions given above, appropriate provisions should be made regarding Special Products and a Special Safeguard Mechanism (SSM) for the developing countries. It has already been decided in the Hong Kong Ministerial Declaration that the Special Products will be self-designated by the developing countries. As the objective is to take care of food security, livelihood security and rural development in the developing countries, the products selected should be adequate in number and the treatment to be accorded to them should allow adequate flexibility regarding protection, through both tariffs and direct quantitative restrictions, as well as support through subsidies.

The SSM should have simple criteria based on a rise in imports or fall in price in the previous year. The SSM measure should be in the form of an additional tariff or a quantitative restriction.

## *NAMA*

The Doha Declaration and the July 04 decision have provided for "less than full reciprocity" for the developing countries in respect of reduction of industrial tariffs. The most appropriate manner in which this objective can be achieved is for the developing countries to open their markets for the developed countries to a lesser degree than the developed countries' opening of their markets for the developing countries.

One way of achieving this is through having an appropriate differential in the reduction in absolute tariff numbers between the developing countries and the developed countries. For example, if the developed countries reduce the tariff from 10 percent to 4 percent (a reduction of 6 in the absolute tariff number), the developing countries could reduce their tariff from 35 percent to 31 percent (a reduction of 4 in the absolute tariff number). The respective coefficients in the Swiss formula for the developed countries and the developing countries then work out accordingly as 6.7 and 271.

Another way may be to lay down differential rates of tariff reduction for the developing countries and the developed countries. For example, the developed countries and the developing countries may reduce their tariffs respectively by 60 percent and 40 percent. In order to have such reduction in their respective tariffs of 4 percent and 30 percent (which are near their respective average industrial-tariff levels), the coefficients for the developed countries and the developing countries respectively should be 2.7 and 45.

These examples show that the coefficients of 10 and 20-30 (for developed and developing countries respectively) which were under consideration in the G6 towards the end of July 2006 are totally out of place. It is therefore necessary to reorient the negotiations in a basic way. The primary focus should not be the coefficients in the Swiss formula; rather, it should be the reduction in absolute tariff numbers or the percentage reduction in tariffs. Then appropriate coefficients should be worked out in order to have the desired reduction.

## *SERVICES*

The developing countries have much less supply capacity in the services sectors compared to the developed countries. Thus they have much less export interest than the developed countries in this area. And wherever the developing countries do have supply capacity and export interest, the developed countries are most reluctant to liberalize.

The foremost interest of the developing countries is in liberalization in Mode 4 (supply of service by movement of persons), which gets constrained in the developed countries on the grounds of immigration policy. Besides, the developed countries also often use qualification and quality standards which the service providers of the developing countries find difficult to meet.

In this background, the objective of the developing countries should be to fully balance their commitments with the benefits they get from the commitments of the developed countries.

Thus, for example, any commitment by the developing countries in any plurilateral sectoral negotiation should be undertaken only when they get a commensurate commitment from the developed countries regarding their liberalization in Mode 4 and their adoption of reasonable standards appropriate to the developing countries' supply capability.

The developing countries should work out a monitoring mechanism for balancing their commitments in various plurilateral/request-offer negotiations with the benefits they get from the commitments of the developed countries.

### *SUBJECTS OF SPECIAL INTEREST TO DEVELOPING COUNTRIES*

In addition to the above areas, it is also important that the subjects that had been sponsored by the developing countries are brought back to the centrestage of the negotiations. There has been a constant tendency in the recent negotiations to push them into the background. These subjects are, in particular, special and differential treatment to developing countries, implementation issues and non-tariff barriers. It may be desirable for the developing countries to link the progress of negotiations on these three subjects with the progress in the areas of agriculture, NAMA and services. They may establish a mechanism to monitor this link regularly and periodically.

### *NEGOTIATING FORMAT*

With the recognition that the restricted and non-transparent negotiating format in the WTO has failed, efforts should be made to follow an inclusive and transparent negotiating process. The strategy of first forging agreement among a limited group of "important" and vocal countries and then expanding the circle of agreement should be given up. No country should have grounds to feel aggrieved because of non-involvement in the negotiations. If getting agreements in open meetings with 150 participants is deemed impractical, the solution does not lie in the arbitrary selection of a few Members to thrash out a deal while leaving out the rest. Some innovative negotiating formats will have to be worked out. Serious work on this in the WTO appears to be a priority task.

## Endnotes

1 For details of other major trade negotiations, see Bhagirath Lal Das (2003), *The WTO and the Multilateral Trading System: Past, Present and Future*, London and New York: Zed Books, Penang: Third World Network, pp. 3-8.

2 For details on the Singapore issues, see Das (2003), op. cit., Chapter IV ("New Issues in the WTO"), and Martin Khor, "The 'Singapore Issues' in the WTO: Implications and Recent Developments", paper distributed at the Asia-Pacific Conference on Trade: Contributing to Growth, Poverty Reduction and Human Development, Penang, Malaysia, 22-24 November 2004. The latter paper may be obtained from the Third World Network <twnet@po.jaring.my>.

3 For details of the inequities, imbalances and deficiencies in the WTO agreements and of the unsatisfactory workings of the WTO decision-making process and negotiating process, see Bhagirath Lal Das (1998), *The WTO Agreements: Deficiencies, Imbalances and Required Changes*, London and New York: Zed Books, Penang: Third World Network, and Das (2003), op. cit., Chapters III and V.

4 For the specific legal provisions of the WTO agreements on agriculture and other subjects, see the texts of the respective agreements in *The Results of the Uruguay Round of Multilateral Trade Negotiations: The Legal Texts*, Geneva: WTO, Cambridge: Cambridge University Press, 1999. For explanations of various provisions of the agreements, see the respective chapters in Bhagirath Lal Das (1999), *The World Trade Organisation: A Guide to the Framework for International Trade*, London and New York: Zed Books, Penang: Third World Network.

5 The Hong Kong Ministerial Conference of the WTO (December 2005) decided that export subsidies would be eliminated by the end of 2013.

6 The Hong Kong Ministerial Conference (December 2005) decided that there would be three bands for reduction in the total trade-distorting support, with higher linear cuts in higher bands. The decision also implies (though the names of the countries are not explicitly mentioned) that the EU will be placed in the top band, the US and Japan in the middle band, and all others, including the developing countries, in the bottom band.

7 The Hong Kong Ministerial Conference decision mentioned in endnote 6 is also applicable to the AMS.

8 The Hong Kong Ministerial Conference (December 2005) decided that the developing countries with no AMS commitments would be exempt from reduction in *de minimis* subsidies.

9 The Hong Kong Ministerial Conference (December 2005) decided that the developing countries would have the flexibility to self-designate an appropriate number of tariff lines as Special Products guided by indicators based on the criteria of food security, livelihood security and rural development.

10 For details, see Das (1998), op. cit.; Bhagirath Lal Das (2001), *WTO Agreement on Agriculture: Deficiencies and Proposals for Change*, Trade & Development

Series No. 17, Penang: Third World Network; and Bhagirath Lal Das (2002), *Some Suggestions for Modalities in Agriculture Negotiations*, Trade & Development Series No. 18, Penang: Third World Network.

11 The Hong Kong Ministerial Conference (December 2005) adopted the Swiss formula for tariff reduction, with the coefficients to be decided later.

12 The Hong Kong Ministerial Conference (December 2005) adopted a non-linear mark-up approach to establish base rates for commencing tariff reductions in the case of currently unbound tariff lines. This implies that there will be full binding coverage for the developing countries.

13 For details of various aspects of the NAMA negotiations, see also Martin Khor and Goh Chien Yen, "The WTO Negotiations on Non-Agricultural Market Access: A Development Perspective", paper distributed at the Asia-Pacific Conference on Trade: Contributing to Growth, Poverty Reduction and Human Development, Penang, Malaysia, 22-24 November 2004. This paper may be obtained from the Third World Network <twnet@po.jaring.my>.

14 The Hong Kong Ministerial Conference (December 2005) decided to intensify negotiations in accordance with the objectives and approaches given in Annex C, which calls for commitments at the current levels of market access in respect of Modes 1 and 2 and enhanced levels of foreign equity participation as well as substantially reduced levels of economic needs tests in respect of Mode 3. Simultaneously it also stipulates appropriate flexibility for individual developing countries as provided for in Article XIX of the GATS.

15 For a historical background of and other details on the implementation issues, see Srinivasan Narayanan, "Implementation Related Issues and Concerns in the WTO", paper distributed at the Asia-Pacific Conference on Trade: Contributing to Growth, Poverty Reduction and Human Development, Penang, Malaysia, 22-24 November 2004.

16 See also United Nations Conference on Trade and Development (UNCTAD) (2000), *Positive Agenda and Future Trade Negotiations,* New York and Geneva: United Nations.

# ANNEX 1

## DOHA MINISTERIAL DECLARATION

*Adopted by the Doha Ministerial Conference on 14 November 2001*

1. The multilateral trading system embodied in the World Trade Organization has contributed significantly to economic growth, development and employment throughout the past fifty years. We are determined, particularly in the light of the global economic slowdown, to maintain the process of reform and liberalization of trade policies, thus ensuring that the system plays its full part in promoting recovery, growth and development. We therefore strongly reaffirm the principles and objectives set out in the Marrakesh Agreement Establishing the World Trade Organization, and pledge to reject the use of protectionism.

2. International trade can play a major role in the promotion of economic development and the alleviation of poverty. We recognize the need for all our peoples to benefit from the increased opportunities and welfare gains that the multilateral trading system generates. The majority of WTO Members are developing countries. We seek to place their needs and interests at the heart of the Work Programme adopted in this Declaration. Recalling the Preamble to the Marrakesh Agreement, we shall continue to make positive efforts designed to ensure that developing countries, and especially the least-developed among them, secure a share in the growth of world trade commensurate with the needs of their economic development. In this context, enhanced market access, balanced rules, and well targeted, sustainably financed technical assistance and capacity-building programmes have important roles to play.

3. We recognize the particular vulnerability of the least-developed countries and the special structural difficulties they face in the global economy. We are committed to addressing the marginalization of least-developed countries in international trade and to improving their effective participation in the multilateral trading system. We recall the commitments made by Ministers at our meetings in Marrakesh, Singapore and Geneva, and by the international community at the Third UN Conference on Least-Developed Countries in Brussels, to help least-developed countries secure beneficial and meaningful integration into the multilateral trading system and the global economy. We are determined that the WTO will play its part in building effectively on these commitments under the Work Programme we are establishing.

4. We stress our commitment to the WTO as the unique forum for global trade rule-making and liberalization, while also recognizing that regional trade agreements can play an important role in promoting the liberalization and expansion of trade and in fostering development.

5. We are aware that the challenges Members face in a rapidly changing international environment cannot be addressed through measures taken in the trade field alone.

We shall continue to work with the Bretton Woods institutions for greater coherence in global economic policy-making.

6. We strongly reaffirm our commitment to the objective of sustainable development, as stated in the Preamble to the Marrakesh Agreement. We are convinced that the aims of upholding and safeguarding an open and non-discriminatory multilateral trading system, and acting for the protection of the environment and the promotion of sustainable development can and must be mutually supportive. We take note of the efforts by Members to conduct national environmental assessments of trade policies on a voluntary basis. We recognize that under WTO rules no country should be prevented from taking measures for the protection of human, animal or plant life or health, or of the environment at the levels it considers appropriate, subject to the requirement that they are not applied in a manner which would constitute a means of arbitrary or unjustifiable discrimination between countries where the same conditions prevail, or a disguised restriction on international trade, and are otherwise in accordance with the provisions of the WTO Agreements. We welcome the WTO´s continued cooperation with UNEP and other inter-governmental environmental organizations. We encourage efforts to promote cooperation between the WTO and relevant international environmental and developmental organizations, especially in the lead-up to the World Summit on Sustainable Development to be held in Johannesburg, South Africa, in September 2002.

7. We reaffirm the right of Members under the General Agreement on Trade in Services to regulate, and to introduce new regulations on, the supply of services.

8. We reaffirm our declaration made at the Singapore Ministerial Conference regarding internationally recognized core labour standards. We take note of work under way in the International Labour Organization (ILO) on the social dimension of globalization.

9. We note with particular satisfaction that this Conference has completed the WTO accession procedures for China and Chinese Taipei. We also welcome the accession as new Members, since our last Session, of Albania, Croatia, Georgia, Jordan, Lithuania, Moldova and Oman, and note the extensive market-access commitments already made by these countries on accession. These accessions will greatly strengthen the multilateral trading system, as will those of the 28 countries now negotiating their accession. We therefore attach great importance to concluding accession proceedings as quickly as possible. In particular, we are committed to accelerating the accession of least-developed countries.

10. Recognizing the challenges posed by an expanding WTO membership, we confirm our collective responsibility to ensure internal transparency and the effective participation of all Members. While emphasizing the intergovernmental character of the organization, we are committed to making the WTO's operations more transparent, including through more effective and prompt dissemination of information, and to improve dialogue with the public. We shall therefore at the

national and multilateral levels continue to promote a better public understanding of the WTO and to communicate the benefits of a liberal, rules-based multilateral trading system.

11. In view of these considerations, we hereby agree to undertake the broad and balanced Work Programme set out below. This incorporates both an expanded negotiating agenda and other important decisions and activities necessary to address the challenges facing the multilateral trading system.

## WORK PROGRAMME

### Implementation-Related Issues and Concerns

12. We attach the utmost importance to the implementation-related issues and concerns raised by Members and are determined to find appropriate solutions to them. In this connection, and having regard to the General Council Decisions of 3 May and 15 December 2000, we further adopt the Decision on Implementation-Related Issues and Concerns in document WT/MIN(01)/17 to address a number of implementation problems faced by Members. We agree that negotiations on outstanding implementation issues shall be an integral part of the Work Programme we are establishing, and that agreements reached at an early stage in these negotiations shall be treated in accordance with the provisions of paragraph 47 below. In this regard, we shall proceed as follows: (a) where we provide a specific negotiating mandate in this Declaration, the relevant implementation issues shall be addressed under that mandate; (b) the other outstanding implementation issues shall be addressed as a matter of priority by the relevant WTO bodies, which shall report to the Trade Negotiations Committee, established under paragraph 46 below, by the end of 2002 for appropriate action.

### Agriculture

13. We recognize the work already undertaken in the negotiations initiated in early 2000 under Article 20 of the Agreement on Agriculture, including the large number of negotiating proposals submitted on behalf of a total of 121 Members. We recall the long-term objective referred to in the Agreement to establish a fair and market-oriented trading system through a programme of fundamental reform encompassing strengthened rules and specific commitments on support and protection in order to correct and prevent restrictions and distortions in world agricultural markets. We reconfirm our commitment to this programme. Building on the work carried out to date and without prejudging the outcome of the negotiations we commit ourselves to comprehensive negotiations aimed at: substantial improvements in market access; reductions of, with a view to phasing out, all forms of export subsidies; and substantial reductions in trade-distorting domestic support. We agree that special and differential treatment for developing countries shall be an integral part of all elements of the negotiations and shall be embodied in the Schedules of concessions and commitments

and as appropriate in the rules and disciplines to be negotiated, so as to be operationally effective and to enable developing countries to effectively take account of their development needs, including food security and rural development. We take note of the non-trade concerns reflected in the negotiating proposals submitted by Members and confirm that non-trade concerns will be taken into account in the negotiations as provided for in the Agreement on Agriculture.

14. Modalities for the further commitments, including provisions for special and differential treatment, shall be established no later than 31 March 2003. Participants shall submit their comprehensive draft Schedules based on these modalities no later than the date of the Fifth Session of the Ministerial Conference. The negotiations, including with respect to rules and disciplines and related legal texts, shall be concluded as part and at the date of conclusion of the negotiating agenda as a whole.

## SERVICES

15. The negotiations on trade in services shall be conducted with a view to promoting the economic growth of all trading partners and the development of developing and least-developed countries. We recognize the work already undertaken in the negotiations, initiated in January 2000 under Article XIX of the General Agreement on Trade in Services, and the large number of proposals submitted by Members on a wide range of sectors and several horizontal issues, as well as on movement of natural persons. We reaffirm the Guidelines and Procedures for the Negotiations adopted by the Council for Trade in Services on 28 March 2001 as the basis for continuing the negotiations, with a view to achieving the objectives of the General Agreement on Trade in Services, as stipulated in the Preamble, Article IV and Article XIX of that Agreement. Participants shall submit initial requests for specific commitments by 30 June 2002 and initial offers by 31 March 2003.

## MARKET ACCESS FOR NON-AGRICULTURAL PRODUCTS

16. We agree to negotiations which shall aim, by modalities to be agreed, to reduce or as appropriate eliminate tariffs, including the reduction or elimination of tariff peaks, high tariffs, and tariff escalation, as well as non-tariff barriers, in particular on products of export interest to developing countries. Product coverage shall be comprehensive and without *a priori* exclusions. The negotiations shall take fully into account the special needs and interests of developing and least-developed country participants, including through less than full reciprocity in reduction commitments, in accordance with the relevant provisions of Article XXVIII *bis* of GATT 1994 and the provisions cited in paragraph 50 below. To this end, the modalities to be agreed will include appropriate studies and capacity-building measures to assist least-developed countries to participate effectively in the negotiations.

## Trade-Related Aspects of Intellectual Property Rights

17. We stress the importance we attach to implementation and interpretation of the Agreement on Trade-Related Aspects of Intellectual Property Rights (TRIPS Agreement) in a manner supportive of public health, by promoting both access to existing medicines and research and development into new medicines and, in this connection, are adopting a separate Declaration.

18. With a view to completing the work started in the Council for Trade-Related Aspects of Intellectual Property Rights (Council for TRIPS) on the implementation of Article 23.4, we agree to negotiate the establishment of a multilateral system of notification and registration of geographical indications for wines and spirits by the Fifth Session of the Ministerial Conference. We note that issues related to the extension of the protection of geographical indications provided for in Article 23 to products other than wines and spirits will be addressed in the Council for TRIPS pursuant to paragraph 12 of this Declaration.

19. We instruct the Council for TRIPS, in pursuing its work programme including under the review of Article 27.3(b), the review of the implementation of the TRIPS Agreement under Article 71.1 and the work foreseen pursuant to paragraph 12 of this Declaration, to examine, *inter alia*, the relationship between the TRIPS Agreement and the Convention on Biological Diversity, the protection of traditional knowledge and folklore, and other relevant new developments raised by Members pursuant to Article 71.1. In undertaking this work, the TRIPS Council shall be guided by the objectives and principles set out in Articles 7 and 8 of the TRIPS Agreement and shall take fully into account the development dimension.

## Relationship between Trade and Investment

20. Recognizing the case for a multilateral framework to secure transparent, stable and predictable conditions for long-term cross-border investment, particularly foreign direct investment, that will contribute to the expansion of trade, and the need for enhanced technical assistance and capacity-building in this area as referred to in paragraph 21, we agree that negotiations will take place after the Fifth Session of the Ministerial Conference on the basis of a decision to be taken, by explicit consensus, at that Session on modalities of negotiations.

21. We recognize the needs of developing and least-developed countries for enhanced support for technical assistance and capacity building in this area, including policy analysis and development so that they may better evaluate the implications of closer multilateral cooperation for their development policies and objectives, and human and institutional development. To this end, we shall work in cooperation with other relevant intergovernmental organizations, including UNCTAD, and through appropriate regional and bilateral channels, to provide strengthened and adequately resourced assistance to respond to these needs.

22. In the period until the Fifth Session, further work in the Working Group on the Relationship Between Trade and Investment will focus on the clarification of: scope and definition; transparency; non-discrimination; modalities for pre-establishment commitments based on a GATS-type, positive list approach; development provisions; exceptions and balance-of-payments safeguards; consultation and the settlement of disputes between Members. Any framework should reflect in a balanced manner the interests of home and host countries, and take due account of the development policies and objectives of host governments as well as their right to regulate in the public interest. The special development, trade and financial needs of developing and least-developed countries should be taken into account as an integral part of any framework, which should enable Members to undertake obligations and commitments commensurate with their individual needs and circumstances. Due regard should be paid to other relevant WTO provisions. Account should be taken, as appropriate, of existing bilateral and regional arrangements on investment.

### Interaction between Trade and Competition Policy

23. Recognizing the case for a multilateral framework to enhance the contribution of competition policy to international trade and development, and the need for enhanced technical assistance and capacity-building in this area as referred to in paragraph 24, we agree that negotiations will take place after the Fifth Session of the Ministerial Conference on the basis of a decision to be taken, by explicit consensus, at that Session on modalities of negotiations.

24. We recognize the needs of developing and least-developed countries for enhanced support for technical assistance and capacity building in this area, including policy analysis and development so that they may better evaluate the implications of closer multilateral cooperation for their development policies and objectives, and human and institutional development. To this end, we shall work in cooperation with other relevant intergovernmental organizations, including UNCTAD, and through appropriate regional and bilateral channels, to provide strengthened and adequately resourced assistance to respond to these needs.

25. In the period until the Fifth Session, further work in the Working Group on the Interaction between Trade and Competition Policy will focus on the clarification of: core principles, including transparency, non-discrimination and procedural fairness, and provisions on hardcore cartels; modalities for voluntary cooperation; and support for progressive reinforcement of competition institutions in developing countries through capacity building. Full account shall be taken of the needs of developing and least-developed country participants and appropriate flexibility provided to address them.

## Transparency in Government Procurement

26. Recognizing the case for a multilateral agreement on transparency in government procurement and the need for enhanced technical assistance and capacity building in this area, we agree that negotiations will take place after the Fifth Session of the Ministerial Conference on the basis of a decision to be taken, by explicit consensus, at that Session on modalities of negotiations. These negotiations will build on the progress made in the Working Group on Transparency in Government Procurement by that time and take into account participants' development priorities, especially those of least-developed country participants. Negotiations shall be limited to the transparency aspects and therefore will not restrict the scope for countries to give preferences to domestic supplies and suppliers. We commit ourselves to ensuring adequate technical assistance and support for capacity building both during the negotiations and after their conclusion.

## Trade Facilitation

27. Recognizing the case for further expediting the movement, release and clearance of goods, including goods in transit, and the need for enhanced technical assistance and capacity building in this area, we agree that negotiations will take place after the Fifth Session of the Ministerial Conference on the basis of a decision to be taken, by explicit consensus, at that Session on modalities of negotiations. In the period until the Fifth Session, the Council for Trade in Goods shall review and as appropriate, clarify and improve relevant aspects of Articles V, VIII and X of the GATT 1994 and identify the trade facilitation needs and priorities of Members, in particular developing and least-developed countries. We commit ourselves to ensuring adequate technical assistance and support for capacity building in this area.

## WTO Rules

28. In the light of experience and of the increasing application of these instruments by Members, we agree to negotiations aimed at clarifying and improving disciplines under the Agreements on Implementation of Article VI of the GATT 1994 and on Subsidies and Countervailing Measures, while preserving the basic concepts, principles and effectiveness of these Agreements and their instruments and objectives, and taking into account the needs of developing and least-developed participants. In the initial phase of the negotiations, participants will indicate the provisions, including disciplines on trade distorting practices, that they seek to clarify and improve in the subsequent phase. In the context of these negotiations, participants shall also aim to clarify and improve WTO disciplines on fisheries subsidies, taking into account the importance of this sector to developing countries. We note that fisheries subsidies are also referred to in paragraph 31.

29. We also agree to negotiations aimed at clarifying and improving disciplines and procedures under the existing WTO provisions applying to regional trade agreements.

The negotiations shall take into account the developmental aspects of regional trade agreements.

### Dispute Settlement Understanding

30. We agree to negotiations on improvements and clarifications of the Dispute Settlement Understanding. The negotiations should be based on the work done thus far as well as any additional proposals by Members, and aim to agree on improvements and clarifications not later than May 2003, at which time we will take steps to ensure that the results enter into force as soon as possible thereafter.

### Trade and Environment

31. With a view to enhancing the mutual supportiveness of trade and environment, we agree to negotiations, without prejudging their outcome, on:

    (i) the relationship between existing WTO rules and specific trade obligations set out in multilateral environmental agreements (MEAs). The negotiations shall be limited in scope to the applicability of such existing WTO rules as among parties to the MEA in question. The negotiations shall not prejudice the WTO rights of any Member that is not a party to the MEA in question;
    (ii) procedures for regular information exchange between MEA Secretariats and the relevant WTO committees, and the criteria for the granting of observer status;
    (iii) the reduction or, as appropriate, elimination of tariff and non-tariff barriers to environmental goods and services.

    We note that fisheries subsidies form part of the negotiations provided for in paragraph 28.

32. We instruct the Committee on Trade and Environment, in pursuing work on all items on its agenda within its current terms of reference, to give particular attention to:

    (i) the effect of environmental measures on market access, especially in relation to developing countries, in particular the least-developed among them, and those situations in which the elimination or reduction of trade restrictions and distortions would benefit trade, the environment and development;
    (ii) the relevant provisions of the Agreement on Trade-Related Aspects of Intellectual Property Rights; and
    (iii) labelling requirements for environmental purposes.

    Work on these issues should include the identification of any need to clarify relevant WTO rules. The Committee shall report to the Fifth Session of the Ministerial Conference, and make recommendations, where appropriate, with respect to future action, including the desirability of negotiations. The outcome of this work as well as the negotiations carried out under paragraph 31(i) and (ii) shall be compatible with the open and non-discriminatory nature of the multilateral trading system, shall not add to or diminish the rights and obligations of Members under existing WTO agreements, in particular the Agreement on the Application of Sanitary and Phytosanitary Measures, nor alter the balance of these rights and obligations, and will take into account the needs of developing and least-developed countries.

33. We recognize the importance of technical assistance and capacity building in the field of trade and environment to developing countries, in particular the least-developed among them. We also encourage that expertise and experience be shared with Members wishing to perform environmental reviews at the national level. A report shall be prepared on these activities for the Fifth Session.

### Electronic Commerce

34. We take note of the work which has been done in the General Council and other relevant bodies since the Ministerial Declaration of 20 May 1998 and agree to continue the Work Programme on Electronic Commerce. The work to date demonstrates that electronic commerce creates new challenges and opportunities for trade for Members at all stages of development, and we recognize the importance of creating and maintaining an environment which is favourable to the future development of electronic commerce. We instruct the General Council to consider the most appropriate institutional arrangements for handling the Work Programme, and to report on further progress to the Fifth Session of the Ministerial Conference. We declare that Members will maintain their current practice of not imposing customs duties on electronic transmissions until the Fifth Session.

### Small Economies

35. We agree to a work programme, under the auspices of the General Council, to examine issues relating to the trade of small economies. The objective of this work is to frame responses to the trade-related issues identified for the fuller integration of small, vulnerable economies into the multilateral trading system, and not to create a sub-category of WTO Members. The General Council shall review the work programme and make recommendations for action to the Fifth Session of the Ministerial Conference.

### Trade, Debt and Finance

36. We agree to an examination, in a Working Group under the auspices of the General Council, of the relationship between trade, debt and finance, and of any possible recommendations on steps that might be taken within the mandate and competence of the WTO to enhance the capacity of the multilateral trading system to contribute to a durable solution to the problem of external indebtedness of developing and least-developed countries, and to strengthen the coherence of international trade and financial policies, with a view to safeguarding the multilateral trading system from

the effects of financial and monetary instability. The General Council shall report to the Fifth Session of the Ministerial Conference on progress in the examination.

### Trade and Transfer of Technology

37. We agree to an examination, in a Working Group under the auspices of the General Council, of the relationship between trade and transfer of technology, and of any possible recommendations on steps that might be taken within the mandate of the WTO to increase flows of technology to developing countries. The General Council shall report to the Fifth Session of the Ministerial Conference on progress in the examination.

### Technical Cooperation and Capacity Building

38. We confirm that technical cooperation and capacity building are core elements of the development dimension of the multilateral trading system, and we welcome and endorse the New Strategy for WTO Technical Cooperation for Capacity Building, Growth and Integration. We instruct the Secretariat, in coordination with other relevant agencies, to support domestic efforts for mainstreaming trade into national plans for economic development and strategies for poverty reduction. The delivery of WTO technical assistance shall be designed to assist developing and least-developed countries and low-income countries in transition to adjust to WTO rules and disciplines, implement obligations and exercise the rights of membership, including drawing on the benefits of an open, rules-based multilateral trading system. Priority shall also be accorded to small, vulnerable, and transition economies, as well as to Members and Observers without representation in Geneva. We reaffirm our support for the valuable work of the International Trade Centre, which should be enhanced.

39. We underscore the urgent necessity for the effective coordinated delivery of technical assistance with bilateral donors, in the OECD Development Assistance Committee and relevant international and regional intergovernmental institutions, within a coherent policy framework and timetable. In the coordinated delivery of technical assistance, we instruct the Director-General to consult with the relevant agencies, bilateral donors and beneficiaries, to identify ways of enhancing and rationalizing the Integrated Framework for Trade-Related Technical Assistance to Least-Developed Countries and the Joint Integrated Technical Assistance Programme (JITAP).

40. We agree that there is a need for technical assistance to benefit from secure and predictable funding. We therefore instruct the Committee on Budget, Finance and Administration to develop a plan for adoption by the General Council in December 2001 that will ensure long-term funding for WTO technical assistance at an overall level no lower than that of the current year and commensurate with the activities outlined above.

41. We have established firm commitments on technical cooperation and capacity building in various paragraphs in this Ministerial Declaration. We reaffirm these specific commitments contained in paragraphs 16, 21, 24, 26, 27, 33, 38-40, 42 and 43, and also reaffirm the understanding in paragraph 2 on the important role of sustainably financed technical assistance and capacity-building programmes. We instruct the Director-General to report to the Fifth Session of the Ministerial Conference, with an interim report to the General Council in December 2002 on the implementation and adequacy of these commitments in the identified paragraphs.

## Least-Developed Countries

42. We acknowledge the seriousness of the concerns expressed by the least-developed countries (LDCs) in the Zanzibar Declaration adopted by their Ministers in July 2001. We recognize that the integration of the LDCs into the multilateral trading system requires meaningful market access, support for the diversification of their production and export base, and trade-related technical assistance and capacity building. We agree that the meaningful integration of LDCs into the trading system and the global economy will involve efforts by all WTO Members. We commit ourselves to the objective of duty-free, quota-free market access for products originating from LDCs. In this regard, we welcome the significant market access improvements by WTO Members in advance of the Third UN Conference on LDCs (LDC-III), in Brussels, May 2001. We further commit ourselves to consider additional measures for progressive improvements in market access for LDCs. Accession of LDCs remains a priority for the Membership. We agree to work to facilitate and accelerate negotiations with acceding LDCs. We instruct the Secretariat to reflect the priority we attach to LDCs' accessions in the annual plans for technical assistance. We reaffirm the commitments we undertook at LDC-III, and agree that the WTO should take into account, in designing its work programme for LDCs, the trade-related elements of the Brussels Declaration and Programme of Action, consistent with the WTO's mandate, adopted at LDC-III. We instruct the Sub-Committee for Least-Developed Countries to design such a work programme and to report on the agreed work programme to the General Council at its first meeting in 2002.

43. We endorse the Integrated Framework for Trade-Related Technical Assistance to Least-Developed Countries (IF) as a viable model for LDCs' trade development. We urge development partners to significantly increase contributions to the IF Trust Fund and WTO extra-budgetary trust funds in favour of LDCs. We urge the core agencies, in coordination with development partners, to explore the enhancement of the IF with a view to addressing the supply-side constraints of LDCs and the extension of the model to all LDCs, following the review of the IF and the appraisal of the ongoing Pilot Scheme in selected LDCs. We request the Director-General, following coordination with heads of the other agencies, to provide an interim report to the General Council in December 2002 and a full report to the Fifth Session of the Ministerial Conference on all issues affecting LDCs.

### Special and Differential Treatment

44. We reaffirm that provisions for special and differential treatment are an integral part of the WTO Agreements. We note the concerns expressed regarding their operation in addressing specific constraints faced by developing countries, particularly least-developed countries. In that connection, we also note that some Members have proposed a Framework Agreement on Special and Differential Treatment (WT/GC/W/442). We therefore agree that all special and differential treatment provisions shall be reviewed with a view to strengthening them and making them more precise, effective and operational. In this connection, we endorse the work programme on special and differential treatment set out in the Decision on Implementation-Related Issues and Concerns.

## ORGANIZATION AND MANAGEMENT OF THE WORK PROGRAMME

45. The negotiations to be pursued under the terms of this Declaration shall be concluded not later than 1 January 2005. The Fifth Session of the Ministerial Conference will take stock of progress in the negotiations, provide any necessary political guidance, and take decisions as necessary. When the results of the negotiations in all areas have been established, a Special Session of the Ministerial Conference will be held to take decisions regarding the adoption and implementation of those results.

46. The overall conduct of the negotiations shall be supervised by a Trade Negotiations Committee under the authority of the General Council. The Trade Negotiations Committee shall hold its first meeting not later than 31 January 2002. It shall establish appropriate negotiating mechanisms as required and supervise the progress of the negotiations.

47. With the exception of the improvements and clarifications of the Dispute Settlement Understanding, the conduct, conclusion and entry into force of the outcome of the negotiations shall be treated as parts of a single undertaking. However, agreements reached at an early stage may be implemented on a provisional or a definitive basis. Early agreements shall be taken into account in assessing the overall balance of the negotiations.

48. Negotiations shall be open to:

(i) all Members of the WTO; and
(ii) States and separate customs territories currently in the process of accession and those that inform Members, at a regular meeting of the General Council, of their intention to negotiate the terms of their membership and for whom an accession working party is established.

Decisions on the outcomes of the negotiations shall be taken only by WTO Members.

49. The negotiations shall be conducted in a transparent manner among participants, in order to facilitate the effective participation of all. They shall be conducted with a view to ensuring benefits to all participants and to achieving an overall balance in the outcome of the negotiations.

50. The negotiations and the other aspects of the Work Programme shall take fully into account the principle of special and differential treatment for developing and least-developed countries embodied in: Part IV of the GATT 1994; the Decision of 28 November 1979 on Differential and More Favourable Treatment, Reciprocity and Fuller Participation of Developing Countries; the Uruguay Round Decision on Measures in Favour of Least-Developed Countries; and all other relevant WTO provisions.

51. The Committee on Trade and Development and the Committee on Trade and Environment shall, within their respective mandates, each act as a forum to identify and debate developmental and environmental aspects of the negotiations, in order to help achieve the objective of having sustainable development appropriately reflected.

52. Those elements of the Work Programme which do not involve negotiations are also accorded a high priority. They shall be pursued under the overall supervision of the General Council, which shall report on progress to the Fifth Session of the Ministerial Conference.

# ANNEX 2

## GENERAL COUNCIL DECISION OF 1 AUGUST 2004

1. The General Council reaffirms the Ministerial Declarations and Decisions adopted at Doha and the full commitment of all Members to give effect to them. The Council emphasizes Members' resolve to complete the Doha Work Programme fully and to conclude successfully the negotiations launched at Doha. Taking into account the Ministerial Statement adopted at Cancún on 14 September 2003, and the statements by the Council Chairman and the Director-General at the Council meeting of 15-16 December 2003, the Council takes note of the report by the Chairman of the Trade Negotiations Committee (TNC) and agrees to take action as follows:

   **a.** **Agriculture**: the General Council adopts the framework set out in Annex A to this document.

   **b.** **Cotton**: the General Council reaffirms the importance of the Sectoral Initiative on Cotton and takes note of the parameters set out in Annex A within which the trade-related aspects of this issue will be pursued in the agriculture negotiations. The General Council also attaches importance to the development aspects of the Cotton Initiative and wishes to stress the complementarity between the trade and development aspects. The Council takes note of the recent Workshop on Cotton in Cotonou on 23-24 March 2004 organized by the WTO Secretariat, and other bilateral and multilateral efforts to make progress on the development assistance aspects and instructs the Secretariat to continue to work with the development community and to provide the Council with periodic reports on relevant developments.

   Members should work on related issues of development multilaterally with the international financial institutions, continue their bilateral programmes, and all developed countries are urged to participate. In this regard, the General Council instructs the Director General to consult with the relevant international organizations, including the Bretton Woods Institutions, the Food and Agriculture Organization and the International Trade Centre to direct effectively existing programmes and any additional resources towards development of the economies where cotton has vital importance.

   **c.** **Non-agricultural Market Access**: the General Council adopts the framework set out in Annex B to this document.

   **d.** **Development**:

   **Principles**: development concerns form an integral part of the Doha Ministerial Declaration. The General Council rededicates and recommits Members to fulfilling the development dimension of the Doha Development Agenda, which places the needs and interests of developing and least-developed countries at the heart of the Doha Work Programme. The Council reiterates the important role that enhanced market access, balanced rules, and well targeted, sustainably financed technical assistance and capacity building programmes can play in the economic development of these countries.

**Special and Differential Treatment**: the General Council reaffirms that provisions for special and differential (S&D) treatment are an integral part of the WTO Agreements. The Council recalls Ministers' decision in Doha to review all S&D treatment provisions with a view to strengthening them and making them more precise, effective and operational. The Council recognizes the progress that has been made so far. The Council instructs the Committee on Trade and Development in Special Session to expeditiously complete the review of all the outstanding Agreement-specific proposals and report to the General Council, with clear recommendations for a decision, by July 2005. The Council further instructs the Committee, within the parameters of the Doha mandate, to address all other outstanding work, including on the cross-cutting issues, the monitoring mechanism and the incorporation of S&D treatment into the architecture of WTO rules, as referred to in TN/CTD/7 and report, as appropriate, to the General Council.

The Council also instructs all WTO bodies to which proposals in Category II have been referred to expeditiously complete the consideration of these proposals and report to the General Council, with clear recommendations for a decision, as soon as possible and no later than July 2005. In doing so these bodies will ensure that, as far as possible, their meetings do not overlap so as to enable full and effective participation of developing countries in these discussions.

**Technical Assistance**: the General Council recognizes the progress that has been made since the Doha Ministerial Conference in expanding Trade-Related Technical Assistance (TRTA) to developing countries and low-income countries in transition. In furthering this effort the Council affirms that such countries, and in particular least-developed countries, should be provided with enhanced TRTA and capacity building, to increase their effective participation in the negotiations, to facilitate their implementation of WTO rules, and to enable them to adjust and diversify their economies. In this context the Council welcomes and further encourages the improved coordination with other agencies, including under the Integrated Framework for TRTA for the LDCs (IF) and the Joint Integrated Technical Assistance Programme (JITAP).

**Implementation**: concerning implementation-related issues, the General Council reaffirms the mandates Ministers gave in paragraph 12 of the Doha Ministerial Declaration and the Doha Decision on Implementation-Related Issues and Concerns, and renews Members' determination to find appropriate solutions to outstanding issues. The Council instructs the Trade Negotiations Committee, negotiating bodies and other WTO bodies concerned to redouble their efforts to find appropriate solutions as a priority. Without prejudice to the positions of Members, the Council requests the Director-General to continue with his consultative process on all outstanding implementation issues under paragraph 12(b) of the Doha Ministerial Declaration, including on issues related to the extension of the protection of geographical indications provided for in Article 23 of the TRIPS Agreement to products other than wines and spirits, if need be by appointing Chairpersons of concerned WTO bodies as his Friends and/or by holding dedicated consultations. The Director-General shall report to the TNC and the General Council no later than May 2005. The Council shall review progress and take any appropriate action no later than July 2005.

**Other Development Issues**: in the ongoing market access negotiations, recognising the fundamental principles of the WTO and relevant provisions of GATT 1994, special attention shall be given to the specific trade and development related needs and concerns of developing countries, including capacity constraints. These particular concerns of developing countries, including relating to food security, rural development, livelihood, preferences, commodities and net food imports, as well as prior unilateral liberalisation, should be taken into consideration, as appropriate, in the course of the Agriculture and NAMA negotiations. The trade-related issues identified for the fuller integration of small, vulnerable economies into the multilateral trading system, should also be addressed, without creating a sub-category of Members, as part of a work programme, as mandated in paragraph 35 of the Doha Ministerial Declaration.

**Least-Developed Countries**: the General Council reaffirms the commitments made at Doha concerning least-developed countries and renews its determination to fulfil these commitments. Members will continue to take due account of the concerns of least-developed countries in the negotiations. The Council confirms that nothing in this Decision shall detract in any way from the special provisions agreed by Members in respect of these countries.

e. **Services**: the General Council takes note of the report to the TNC by the Special Session of the Council for Trade in Services[1] and reaffirms Members' commitment to progress in this area of the negotiations in line with the Doha mandate. The Council adopts the recommendations agreed by the Special Session, set out in Annex C to this document, on the basis of which further progress in the services negotiations will be pursued. Revised offers should be tabled by May 2005.

f. **Other negotiating bodies**:

**Rules, Trade & Environment and TRIPS**: the General Council takes note of the reports to the TNC by the Negotiating Group on Rules and by the Special

[1] This report is contained in document TN/S/16.

Sessions of the Committee on Trade and Environment and the TRIPS Council.[2] The Council reaffirms Members' commitment to progress in all of these areas of the negotiations in line with the Doha mandates.

**Dispute Settlement**: the General Council takes note of the report to the TNC by the Special Session of the Dispute Settlement Body[3] and reaffirms Members' commitment to progress in this area of the negotiations in line with the Doha mandate. The Council adopts the TNC's recommendation that work in the Special Session should continue on the basis set out by the Chairman of that body in his report to the TNC.

g. **Trade Facilitation**: taking note of the work done on trade facilitation by the Council for Trade in Goods under the mandate in paragraph 27 of the Doha Ministerial Declaration and the work carried out under the auspices of the General Council both prior to the Fifth Ministerial Conference and after its conclusion, the General Council decides by explicit consensus to commence negotiations on the basis of the modalities set out in Annex D to this document.

**Relationship between Trade and Investment, Interaction between Trade and Competition Policy and Transparency in Government Procurement**: the Council agrees that these issues, mentioned in the Doha Ministerial Declaration in paragraphs 20-22, 23-25 and 26 respectively, will not form part of the Work Programme set out in that Declaration and therefore no work towards negotiations on any of these issues will take place within the WTO during the Doha Round.

h. **Other elements of the Work Programme**: the General Council reaffirms the high priority Ministers at Doha gave to those elements of the Work Programme which do not involve negotiations. Noting that a number of these issues are of particular interest to developing-country Members, the Council emphasizes its commitment to fulfil the mandates given by Ministers in all these areas. To this end, the General Council and other relevant bodies shall report in line with their Doha mandates to the Sixth Session of the Ministerial Conference. The moratoria covered by paragraph 11.1 of the Doha Ministerial Decision on Implementation-related Issues and Concerns and paragraph 34 of the Doha Ministerial Declaration are extended up to the Sixth Ministerial Conference.

2. The General Council agrees that this Decision and its Annexes shall not be used in any dispute settlement proceeding under the DSU and shall not be used for interpreting the existing WTO Agreements.

3. The General Council calls on all Members to redouble their efforts towards the conclusion of a balanced overall outcome of the Doha Development Agenda in

2 The reports to the TNC referenced in this paragraph are contained in the following documents: Negotiating Group on Rules – TN/RL/9; Special Session of the Committee on Trade and Environment – TN/TE/9; Special Session of the Council for TRIPS – TN/IP/10.

3 This report is contained in document TN/DS/10.

fulfilment of the commitments Ministers took at Doha. The Council agrees to continue the negotiations launched at Doha beyond the timeframe set out in paragraph 45 of the Doha Declaration, leading to the Sixth Session of the Ministerial Conference. Recalling its decision of 21 October 2003 to accept the generous offer of the Government of Hong Kong, China to host the Sixth Session, the Council further agrees that this Session will be held in December 2005.

---

## ANNEX A

## FRAMEWORK FOR ESTABLISHING MODALITIES IN AGRICULTURE

1. The starting point for the current phase of the agriculture negotiations has been the mandate set out in Paragraph 13 of the Doha Ministerial Declaration. This in turn built on the long-term objective of the Agreement on Agriculture to establish a fair and market-oriented trading system through a programme of fundamental reform. The elements below offer the additional precision required at this stage of the negotiations and thus the basis for the negotiations of full modalities in the next phase. The level of ambition set by the Doha mandate will continue to be the basis for the negotiations on agriculture.

2. The final balance will be found only at the conclusion of these subsequent negotiations and within the Single Undertaking. To achieve this balance, the modalities to be developed will need to incorporate operationally effective and meaningful provisions for special and differential treatment for developing country Members. Agriculture is of critical importance to the economic development of developing country Members and they must be able to pursue agricultural policies that are supportive of their development goals, poverty reduction strategies, food security and livelihood concerns. Non-trade concerns, as referred to in Paragraph 13 of the Doha Declaration, will be taken into account.

3. The reforms in all three pillars form an interconnected whole and must be approached in a balanced and equitable manner.

4. The General Council recognizes the importance of cotton for a certain number of countries and its vital importance for developing countries, especially LDCs. It will be addressed ambitiously, expeditiously, and specifically, within the agriculture negotiations. The provisions of this framework provide a basis for this approach, as does the sectoral initiative on cotton. The Special Session of the Committee on Agriculture shall ensure appropriate prioritization of the cotton issue independently from other sectoral initiatives. A subcommittee on cotton will meet periodically and report to the Special Session of the Committee on Agriculture to review progress. Work shall encompass all trade-distorting policies affecting the sector in all three pillars of market access, domestic support, and export competition, as specified in the Doha text and this Framework text.

5. Coherence between trade and development aspects of the cotton issue will be pursued as set out in paragraph 1.b of the text to which this Framework is annexed.

## DOMESTIC SUPPORT

6. The Doha Ministerial Declaration calls for "substantial reductions in trade-distorting domestic support". With a view to achieving these substantial reductions, the negotiations in this pillar will ensure the following:

- Special and differential treatment remains an integral component of domestic support. Modalities to be developed will include longer implementation periods and lower reduction coefficients for all types of trade-distorting domestic support and continued access to the provisions under Article 6.2.

- There will be a strong element of harmonisation in the reductions made by developed Members. Specifically, higher levels of permitted trade-distorting domestic support will be subject to deeper cuts.

- Each such Member will make a substantial reduction in the overall level of its trade-distorting support from bound levels.

- As well as this overall commitment, Final Bound Total AMS and permitted *de minimis* levels will be subject to substantial reductions and, in the case of the Blue Box, will be capped as specified in paragraph 15 in order to ensure results that are coherent with the long-term reform objective. Any clarification or development of rules and conditions to govern trade distorting support will take this into account.

### *Overall Reduction: A Tiered Formula*

7. The overall base level of all trade-distorting domestic support, as measured by the Final Bound Total AMS plus permitted *de minimis* level and the level agreed in paragraph 8 below for Blue Box payments, will be reduced according to a tiered formula. Under this formula, Members having higher levels of trade-distorting domestic support will make greater overall reductions in order to achieve a harmonizing result. As the first instalment of the overall cut, in the first year and throughout the implementation period, the sum of all trade-distorting support will not exceed 80 per cent of the sum of Final Bound Total AMS plus permitted *de minimis* plus the Blue Box at the level determined in paragraph 15.

8. The following parameters will guide the further negotiation of this tiered formula:

- This commitment will apply as a minimum overall commitment. It will not be applied as a ceiling on reductions of overall trade-distorting domestic support, should the separate and complementary formulae to be developed for Total

AMS, *de minimis* and Blue Box payments imply, when taken together, a deeper cut in overall trade-distorting domestic support for an individual Member.

- The base for measuring the Blue Box component will be the higher of existing Blue Box payments during a recent representative period to be agreed and the cap established in paragraph 15 below.

***Final Bound Total AMS: A Tiered Formula***

9. To achieve reductions with a harmonizing effect:

- Final Bound Total AMS will be reduced substantially, using a tiered approach.

- Members having higher Total AMS will make greater reductions.

- To prevent circumvention of the objective of the Agreement through transfers of unchanged domestic support between different support categories, product-specific AMSs will be capped at their respective average levels according to a methodology to be agreed.

- Substantial reductions in Final Bound Total AMS will result in reductions of some product-specific support.

10. Members may make greater than formula reductions in order to achieve the required level of cut in overall trade-distorting domestic support.

***De Minimis***

11. Reductions in *de minimis* will be negotiated taking into account the principle of special and differential treatment. Developing countries that allocate almost all *de minimis* support for subsistence and resource-poor farmers will be exempt.

12. Members may make greater than formula reductions in order to achieve the required level of cut in overall trade-distorting domestic support.

***Blue Box***

13. Members recognize the role of the Blue Box in promoting agricultural reforms. In this light, Article 6.5 will be reviewed so that Members may have recourse to the following measures:

- Direct payments under production-limiting programmes if:
  - such payments are based on fixed and unchanging areas and yields; or
  - such payments are made on 85% or less of a fixed and unchanging base level of production; or

- livestock payments are made on a fixed and unchanging number of head.

Or

- Direct payments that do not require production if:
  - such payments are based on fixed and unchanging bases and yields; or
  - livestock payments made on a fixed and unchanging number of head; and
  - such payments are made on 85% or less of a fixed and unchanging base level of production.

14. The above criteria, along with additional criteria will be negotiated. Any such criteria will ensure that Blue Box payments are less trade-distorting than AMS measures, it being understood that:

- Any new criteria would need to take account of the balance of WTO rights and obligations.

- Any new criteria to be agreed will not have the perverse effect of undoing ongoing reforms.

15. Blue Box support will not exceed 5% of a Member's average total value of agricultural production during an historical period. The historical period will be established in the negotiations. This ceiling will apply to any actual or potential Blue Box user from the beginning of the implementation period. In cases where a Member has placed an exceptionally large percentage of its trade-distorting support in the Blue Box, some flexibility will be provided on a basis to be agreed to ensure that such a Member is not called upon to make a wholly disproportionate cut.

***Green Box***

16. Green Box criteria will be reviewed and clarified with a view to ensuring that Green Box measures have no, or at most minimal, trade-distorting effects or effects on production. Such a review and clarification will need to ensure that the basic concepts, principles and effectiveness of the Green Box remain and take due account of non-trade concerns. The improved obligations for monitoring and surveillance of all new disciplines foreshadowed in paragraph 48 below will be particularly important with respect to the Green Box.

## EXPORT COMPETITION

17. The Doha Ministerial Declaration calls for "reduction of, with a view to phasing out, all forms of export subsidies". As an outcome of the negotiations, Members agree to establish detailed modalities ensuring the parallel elimination of all forms of export subsidies and disciplines on all export measures with equivalent effect by a credible end date.

*End Point*

18. The following will be eliminated by the end date to be agreed:

- Export subsidies as scheduled.

- Export credits, export credit guarantees or insurance programmes with repayment periods beyond 180 days.

- Terms and conditions relating to export credits, export credit guarantees or insurance programmes with repayment periods of 180 days and below which are not in accordance with disciplines to be agreed. These disciplines will cover, *inter alia*, payment of interest, minimum interest rates, minimum premium requirements, and other elements which can constitute subsidies or otherwise distort trade.

- Trade distorting practices with respect to exporting STEs including eliminating export subsidies provided to or by them, government financing, and the underwriting of losses. The issue of the future use of monopoly powers will be subject to further negotiation.

- Provision of food aid that is not in conformity with operationally effective disciplines to be agreed. The objective of such disciplines will be to prevent commercial displacement. The role of international organizations as regards the provision of food aid by Members, including related humanitarian and developmental issues, will be addressed in the negotiations. The question of providing food aid exclusively in fully grant form will also be addressed in the negotiations.

19. Effective transparency provisions for paragraph 18 will be established. Such provisions, in accordance with standard WTO practice, will be consistent with commercial confidentiality considerations.

*Implementation*

20. Commitments and disciplines in paragraph 18 will be implemented according to a schedule and modalities to be agreed. Commitments will be implemented by annual instalments. Their phasing will take into account the need for some coherence with internal reform steps of Members.
21. The negotiation of the elements in paragraph 18 and their implementation will ensure equivalent and parallel commitments by Members.

*Special and Differential Treatment*

22. Developing country Members will benefit from longer implementation periods for the phasing out of all forms of export subsidies.

23. Developing countries will continue to benefit from special and differential treatment under the provisions of Article 9.4 of the Agreement on Agriculture for a reasonable period, to be negotiated, after the phasing out of all forms of export subsidies and implementation of all disciplines identified above are completed.

24. Members will ensure that the disciplines on export credits, export credit guarantees or insurance programmes to be agreed will make appropriate provision for differential treatment in favour of least-developed and net food-importing developing countries as provided for in paragraph 4 of the Decision on Measures Concerning the Possible Negative Effects of the Reform Programme on Least-Developed and Net Food-Importing Developing Countries. Improved obligations for monitoring and surveillance of all new disciplines as foreshadowed in paragraph 48 will be critically important in this regard. Provisions to be agreed in this respect must not undermine the commitments undertaken by Members under the obligations in paragraph 18 above.

25. STEs in developing country Members which enjoy special privileges to preserve domestic consumer price stability and to ensure food security will receive special consideration for maintaining monopoly status.

### *Special Circumstances*

26. In exceptional circumstances, which cannot be adequately covered by food aid, commercial export credits or preferential international financing facilities, ad hoc temporary financing arrangements relating to exports to developing countries may be agreed by Members. Such agreements must not have the effect of undermining commitments undertaken by Members in paragraph 18 above, and will be based on criteria and consultation procedures to be established.

## MARKET ACCESS

27. The Doha Ministerial Declaration calls for "substantial improvements in market access". Members also agreed that special and differential treatment for developing Members would be an integral part of all elements in the negotiations.

### *The Single Approach: a Tiered Formula*

28. To ensure that a single approach for developed and developing country Members meets all the objectives of the Doha mandate, tariff reductions will be made through a tiered formula that takes into account their different tariff structures.

29. To ensure that such a formula will lead to substantial trade expansion, the following principles will guide its further negotiation:

- Tariff reductions will be made from bound rates. Substantial overall tariff reductions will be achieved as a final result from negotiations.

- Each Member (other than LDCs) will make a contribution. Operationally effective special and differential provisions for developing country Members will be an integral part of all elements.

- Progressivity in tariff reductions will be achieved through deeper cuts in higher tariffs with flexibilities for sensitive products. Substantial improvements in market access will be achieved for all products.

30. The number of bands, the thresholds for defining the bands and the type of tariff reduction in each band remain under negotiation. The role of a tariff cap in a tiered formula with distinct treatment for sensitive products will be further evaluated.

***Sensitive Products***

Selection

31. Without undermining the overall objective of the tiered approach, Members may designate an appropriate number, to be negotiated, of tariff lines to be treated as sensitive, taking account of existing commitments for these products.

Treatment

32. The principle of 'substantial improvement' will apply to each product.

33. 'Substantial improvement' will be achieved through combinations of tariff quota commitments and tariff reductions applying to each product. However, balance in this negotiation will be found only if the final negotiated result also reflects the sensitivity of the product concerned.

34. Some MFN-based tariff quota expansion will be required for all such products. A base for such an expansion will be established, taking account of coherent and equitable criteria to be developed in the negotiations. In order not to undermine the objective of the tiered approach, for all such products, MFN based tariff quota expansion will be provided under specific rules to be negotiated taking into account deviations from the tariff formula.

***Other Elements***

35. Other elements that will give the flexibility required to reach a final balanced result include reduction or elimination of in-quota tariff rates, and operationally effective improvements in tariff quota administration for existing tariff quotas so as to enable Members, and particularly developing country Members, to fully benefit from the market access opportunities under tariff rate quotas.

36. Tariff escalation will be addressed through a formula to be agreed.

37. The issue of tariff simplification remains under negotiation.

38. The question of the special agricultural safeguard (SSG) remains under negotiation.

***Special and differential treatment***

39. Having regard to their rural development, food security and/or livelihood security needs, special and differential treatment for developing countries will be an integral part of all elements of the negotiation, including the tariff reduction formula, the number and treatment of sensitive products, expansion of tariff rate quotas, and implementation period.

40. Proportionality will be achieved by requiring lesser tariff reduction commitments or tariff quota expansion commitments from developing country Members.

41. Developing country Members will have the flexibility to designate an appropriate number of products as Special Products, based on criteria of food security, livelihood security and rural development needs. These products will be eligible for more flexible treatment. The criteria and treatment of these products will be further specified during the negotiation phase and will recognize the fundamental importance of Special Products to developing countries.

42. A Special Safeguard Mechanism (SSM) will be established for use by developing country Members.

43. Full implementation of the long-standing commitment to achieve the fullest liberalisation of trade in tropical agricultural products and for products of particular importance to the diversification of production from the growing of illicit narcotic crops is overdue and will be addressed effectively in the market access negotiations.

44. The importance of long-standing preferences is fully recognised. The issue of preference erosion will be addressed. For the further consideration in this regard, paragraph 16 and other relevant provisions of TN/AG/W/1/Rev.1 will be used as a reference.

## LEAST-DEVELOPED COUNTRIES

45. Least-Developed Countries, which will have full access to all special and differential treatment provisions above, are not required to undertake reduction commitments. Developed Members, and developing country Members in a position to do so, should provide duty-free and quota-free market access for products originating from least-developed countries.

46. Work on cotton under all the pillars will reflect the vital importance of this sector to certain LDC Members and we will work to achieve ambitious results expeditiously.

**RECENTLY ACCEDED MEMBERS**

47. The particular concerns of recently acceded Members will be effectively addressed through specific flexibility provisions.

**MONITORING AND SURVEILLANCE**

48. Article 18 of the Agreement on Agriculture will be amended with a view to enhancing monitoring so as to effectively ensure full transparency, including through timely and complete notifications with respect to the commitments in market access, domestic support and export competition. The particular concerns of developing countries in this regard will be addressed.

**OTHER ISSUES**

49. Issues of interest but not agreed: sectoral initiatives, differential export taxes, GIs.

50. Disciplines on export prohibitions and restrictions in Article 12.1 of the Agreement on Agriculture will be strengthened.

---

## ANNEX B

## FRAMEWORK FOR ESTABLISHING MODALITIES IN MARKET ACCESS FOR NON-AGRICULTURAL PRODUCTS

1. This Framework contains the initial elements for future work on modalities by the Negotiating Group on Market Access. Additional negotiations are required to reach agreement on the specifics of some of these elements. These relate to the formula, the issues concerning the treatment of unbound tariffs in indent two of paragraph 5, the flexibilities for developing-country participants, the issue of participation in the sectorial tariff component and the preferences. In order to finalize the modalities, the Negotiating Group is instructed to address these issues expeditiously in a manner consistent with the mandate of paragraph 16 of the Doha Ministerial Declaration and the overall balance therein.

2. We reaffirm that negotiations on market access for non-agricultural products shall aim to reduce or as appropriate eliminate tariffs, including the reduction or elimination

of tariff peaks, high tariffs, and tariff escalation, as well as non-tariff barriers, in particular on products of export interest to developing countries. We also reaffirm the importance of special and differential treatment and less than full reciprocity in reduction commitments as integral parts of the modalities.

3. We acknowledge the substantial work undertaken by the Negotiating Group on Market Access and the progress towards achieving an agreement on negotiating modalities. We take note of the constructive dialogue on the Chair's Draft Elements of Modalities (TN/MA/W/35/Rev.1) and confirm our intention to use this document as a reference for the future work of the Negotiating Group. We instruct the Negotiating Group to continue its work, as mandated by paragraph 16 of the Doha Ministerial Declaration with its corresponding references to the relevant provisions of Article XXVIII *bis* of GATT 1994 and to the provisions cited in paragraph 50 of the Doha Ministerial Declaration, on the basis set out below.

4. We recognize that a formula approach is key to reducing tariffs, and reducing or eliminating tariff peaks, high tariffs, and tariff escalation. We agree that the Negotiating Group should continue its work on a non-linear formula applied on a line-by-line basis which shall take fully into account the special needs and interests of developing and least-developed country participants, including through less than full reciprocity in reduction commitments.

5. We further agree on the following elements regarding the formula:

- product coverage shall be comprehensive without *a priori* exclusions;
- tariff reductions or elimination shall commence from the bound rates after full implementation of current concessions; however, for unbound tariff lines, the basis for commencing the tariff reductions shall be [two] times the MFN applied rate in the base year;
- the base year for MFN applied tariff rates shall be 2001 (applicable rates on 14 November);
- credit shall be given for autonomous liberalization by developing countries provided that the tariff lines were bound on an MFN basis in the WTO since the conclusion of the Uruguay Round;
- all non-*ad valorem* duties shall be converted to *ad valorem* equivalents on the basis of a methodology to be determined and bound in *ad valorem* terms;
- negotiations shall commence on the basis of the HS96 or HS2002 nomenclature, with the results of the negotiations to be finalized in HS2002 nomenclature;
- the reference period for import data shall be 1999-2001.

6. We furthermore agree that, as an exception, participants with a binding coverage of non-agricultural tariff lines of less than [35] percent would be exempt from making tariff reductions through the formula. Instead, we expect them to bind [100] percent

of non-agricultural tariff lines at an average level that does not exceed the overall average of bound tariffs for all developing countries after full implementation of current concessions.

7. We recognize that a sectorial tariff component, aiming at elimination or harmonization is another key element to achieving the objectives of paragraph 16 of the Doha Ministerial Declaration with regard to the reduction or elimination of tariffs, in particular on products of export interest to developing countries. We recognize that participation by all participants will be important to that effect. We therefore instruct the Negotiating Group to pursue its discussions on such a component, with a view to defining product coverage, participation, and adequate provisions of flexibility for developing-country participants.

8. We agree that developing-country participants shall have longer implementation periods for tariff reductions. In addition, they shall be given the following flexibility:

   a) applying less than formula cuts to up to [10] percent of the tariff lines provided that the cuts are no less than half the formula cuts and that these tariff lines do not exceed [10] percent of the total value of a Member's imports; or

   b) keeping, as an exception, tariff lines unbound, or not applying formula cuts for up to [5] percent of tariff lines provided they do not exceed [5] percent of the total value of a Member's imports.

   We furthermore agree that this flexibility could not be used to exclude entire HS Chapters.

9. We agree that least-developed country participants shall not be required to apply the formula nor participate in the sectorial approach, however, as part of their contribution to this round of negotiations, they are expected to substantially increase their level of binding commitments.

10. Furthermore, in recognition of the need to enhance the integration of least-developed countries into the multilateral trading system and support the diversification of their production and export base, we call upon developed-country participants and other participants who so decide, to grant on an autonomous basis duty-free and quota-free market access for non-agricultural products originating from least-developed countries by the year […].

11. We recognize that newly acceded Members shall have recourse to special provisions for tariff reductions in order to take into account their extensive market access commitments undertaken as part of their accession and that staged tariff reductions are still being implemented in many cases. We instruct the Negotiating Group to further elaborate on such provisions.

12. We agree that pending agreement on core modalities for tariffs, the possibilities of supplementary modalities such as zero-for-zero sector elimination, sectorial harmonization, and request & offer, should be kept open.

13. In addition, we ask developed-country participants and other participants who so decide to consider the elimination of low duties.

14. We recognize that NTBs are an integral and equally important part of these negotiations and instruct participants to intensify their work on NTBs. In particular, we encourage all participants to make notifications on NTBs by 31 October 2004 and to proceed with identification, examination, categorization, and ultimately negotiations on NTBs. We take note that the modalities for addressing NTBs in these negotiations could include request/offer, horizontal, or vertical approaches; and should fully take into account the principle of special and differential treatment for developing and least-developed country participants.

15. We recognize that appropriate studies and capacity building measures shall be an integral part of the modalities to be agreed. We also recognize the work that has already been undertaken in these areas and ask participants to continue to identify such issues to improve participation in the negotiations.

16. We recognize the challenges that may be faced by non-reciprocal preference beneficiary Members and those Members that are at present highly dependent on tariff revenue as a result of these negotiations on non-agricultural products. We instruct the Negotiating Group to take into consideration, in the course of its work, the particular needs that may arise for the Members concerned.

17. We furthermore encourage the Negotiating Group to work closely with the Committee on Trade and Environment in Special Session with a view to addressing the issue of non-agricultural environmental goods covered in paragraph 31 (iii) of the Doha Ministerial Declaration.

---

## ANNEX C

## RECOMMENDATIONS OF THE SPECIAL SESSION OF THE COUNCIL FOR TRADE IN SERVICES

(a) Members who have not yet submitted their initial offers must do so as soon as possible.

(b) A date for the submission of a round of revised offers should be established as soon as feasible.

(c) With a view to providing effective market access to all Members and in order to ensure a substantive outcome, Members shall strive to ensure a high quality of offers, particularly in sectors and modes of supply of export interest to developing countries, with special attention to be given to least-developed countries.

(d) Members shall aim to achieve progressively higher levels of liberalization with no *a priori* exclusion of any service sector or mode of supply and shall give special attention to sectors and modes of supply of export interest to developing countries. Members note the interest of developing countries, as well as other Members, in Mode 4.

(e) Members must intensify their efforts to conclude the negotiations on rule-making under GATS Articles VI:4, X, XIII and XV in accordance with their respective mandates and deadlines.

(f) Targeted technical assistance should be provided with a view to enabling developing countries to participate effectively in the negotiations.

(g) For the purpose of the Sixth Ministerial meeting, the Special Session of the Council for Trade in Services shall review progress in these negotiations and provide a full report to the Trade Negotiations Committee, including possible recommendations.

---

## ANNEX D

## MODALITIES FOR NEGOTIATIONS ON TRADE FACILITATION

1. Negotiations shall aim to clarify and improve relevant aspects of Articles V, VIII and X of the GATT 1994 with a view to further expediting the movement, release and clearance of goods, including goods in transit.[1] Negotiations shall also aim at enhancing technical assistance and support for capacity building in this area. The negotiations shall further aim at provisions for effective cooperation between customs or any other appropriate authorities on trade facilitation and customs compliance issues.

2. The results of the negotiations shall take fully into account the principle of special and differential treatment for developing and least-developed countries. Members recognize that this principle should extend beyond the granting of traditional transition periods for implementing commitments. In particular, the extent and the timing of

[1] It is understood that this is without prejudice to the possible format of the final result of the negotiations and would allow consideration of various forms of outcomes.

entering into commitments shall be related to the implementation capacities of developing and least-developed Members. It is further agreed that those Members would not be obliged to undertake investments in infrastructure projects beyond their means.

3. Least-developed country Members will only be required to undertake commitments to the extent consistent with their individual development, financial and trade needs or their administrative and institutional capabilities.

4. As an integral part of the negotiations, Members shall seek to identify their trade facilitation needs and priorities, particularly those of developing and least-developed countries, and shall also address the concerns of developing and least-developed countries related to cost implications of proposed measures.

5. It is recognized that the provision of technical assistance and support for capacity building is vital for developing and least-developed countries to enable them to fully participate in and benefit from the negotiations. Members, in particular developed countries, therefore commit themselves to adequately ensure such support and assistance during the negotiations.[2]

6. Support and assistance should also be provided to help developing and least-developed countries implement the commitments resulting from the negotiations, in accordance with their nature and scope. In this context, it is recognized that negotiations could lead to certain commitments whose implementation would require support for infrastructure development on the part of some Members. In these limited cases, developed-country Members will make every effort to ensure support and assistance directly related to the nature and scope of the commitments in order to allow implementation. It is understood, however, that in cases where required support and assistance for such infrastructure is not forthcoming, and where a developing or least-developed Member continues to lack the necessary capacity, implementation will not be required. While every effort will be made to ensure the necessary support and assistance, it is understood that the commitments by developed countries to provide such support are not open-ended.

7. Members agree to review the effectiveness of the support and assistance provided and its ability to support the implementation of the results of the negotiations.

8. In order to make technical assistance and capacity building more effective and operational and to ensure better coherence, Members shall invite relevant international organizations, including the IMF, OECD, UNCTAD, WCO and the World Bank to undertake a collaborative effort in this regard.

---

[2] In connection with this paragraph, Members note that paragraph 38 of the Doha Ministerial Declaration addresses relevant technical assistance and capacity building concerns of Members.

9. Due account shall be taken of the relevant work of the WCO and other relevant international organizations in this area.

10. Paragraphs 45-51 of the Doha Ministerial Declaration shall apply to these negotiations. At its first meeting after the July session of the General Council, the Trade Negotiations Committee shall establish a Negotiating Group on Trade Facilitation and appoint its Chair. The first meeting of the Negotiating Group shall agree on a work plan and schedule of meetings.

# ANNEX 3

## GUIDELINES AND PROCEDURES FOR THE NEGOTIATIONS ON TRADE IN SERVICES

*Adopted by the Special Session of the Council for Trade in Services on 28 March 2001*

### I. Objectives and Principles

1. Pursuant to the objectives of the GATS, as stipulated in the Preamble and Article IV, and as required by Article XIX, the negotiations shall be conducted on the basis of progressive liberalization as a means of promoting the economic growth of all trading partners and the development of developing countries, and recognizing the right of Members to regulate, and to introduce new regulations, on the supply of services. The negotiations shall aim to achieve progressively higher levels of liberalization of trade in services through the reduction or elimination of the adverse effects on trade in services of measures as a means of providing effective market access, and with a view to promoting the interests of all participants on a mutually advantageous basis and to securing an overall balance of rights and obligations.
2. The negotiations shall aim to increase the participation of developing countries in trade in services. There shall be appropriate flexibility for individual developing country Members, as provided for by Article XIX:2. Special priority shall be granted to least-developed country Members as stipulated in Article IV:3.
3. The process of liberalization shall take place with due respect for national policy objectives, the level of development and the size of economies of individual Members, both overall and in individual sectors. Due consideration should be given to the needs of small and medium-sized service suppliers, particularly those of developing countries.
4. The negotiations shall take place within and shall respect the existing structure and principles of the GATS, including the right to specify sectors in which commitments will be undertaken and the four modes of supply.

### II. Scope

5. There shall be no *a priori* exclusion of any service sector or mode of supply. Special attention shall be given to sectors and modes of supply of export interest to developing countries.
6. MFN Exemptions shall be subject to negotiation according to paragraph 6 of the Annex on Article II (MFN) Exemptions. In such negotiations, appropriate flexibility shall be accorded to individual developing country Members.
7. Negotiations on safeguards under Article X shall be completed by 15 March 2002 according to the Decision adopted by the Council for Trade in Services on 1 December 2000. Members shall aim to complete negotiations under Articles VI:4, XIII and XV prior to the conclusion of negotiations on specific commitments.

## III. Modalities and Procedures

8. The negotiations shall be conducted in Special Sessions of the Council for Trade in Services, which will report on a regular basis to the General Council, in accordance with decisions taken by the General Council.
9. Negotiations shall be transparent and open to all Members and acceding States and separate customs territories according to Decisions taken in this regard by the General Council.
10. The starting point for the negotiation of specific commitments shall be the current schedules, without prejudice to the content of requests.
11. Liberalization shall be advanced through bilateral, plurilateral or multilateral negotiations. The main method of negotiation shall be the request-offer approach.
12. There shall be appropriate flexibility for individual developing country Members for opening fewer sectors, liberalizing fewer types of transactions, progressively extending market access in line with their development situation and, when making access to their markets available to foreign service suppliers, attaching to such access conditions aimed at achieving the objectives referred to in Article IV.
13. Based on multilaterally agreed criteria, account shall be taken and credit shall be given in the negotiations for autonomous liberalization undertaken by Members since previous negotiations. Members shall endeavour to develop such criteria prior to the start of negotiation of specific commitments.
14. The Council for Trade in Services in Special Sessions shall continue to carry out an assessment of trade in services in overall terms and on a sectoral basis with reference to the objectives of the GATS and of Article IV in particular. This shall be an ongoing activity of the Council and negotiations shall be adjusted in the light of the results of the assessment. In accordance with Article XXV of the GATS, technical assistance shall be provided to developing country Members, on request, in order to carry out national/regional assessments.
15. To ensure the effective implementation of Articles IV and XIX:2, the Council for Trade in Services in Special Session, when reviewing progress in negotiations, shall consider the extent to which Article IV is being implemented and suggest ways and means of promoting the goals established therein. In implementing Article IV consideration shall also be given to the needs of small service suppliers of developing countries. It shall also conduct an evaluation, before the completion of the negotiations, of the results attained in terms of the objectives of Article IV.
16. While the Council for Trade in Services in Special Sessions may establish subsidiary bodies as it deems necessary, the proliferation of such bodies should be avoided to the maximum extent possible. Existing subsidiary bodies shall be utilized to their maximum capacity.
17. The needs of smaller delegations should be taken into account, e.g. by scheduling meetings in sequence and not in parallel.
18. The Council for Trade in Services in Special Sessions shall, when appropriate, develop time schedules for the conduct of the negotiations in accordance with any relevant decisions taken by the General Council.

# ANNEX 4

## IMPLEMENTATION-RELATED ISSUES AND CONCERNS

*Doha Ministerial Conference Decision of 14 November 2001 (WT/MIN(01)/17)*

The Ministerial Conference,

*Having regard to* Articles IV.1, IV.5 and IX of the Marrakesh Agreement Establishing the World Trade Organization (WTO);

*Mindful* of the importance that Members attach to the increased participation of developing countries in the multilateral trading system, and of the need to ensure that the system responds fully to the needs and interests of all participants;

*Determined* to take concrete action to address issues and concerns that have been raised by many developing-country Members regarding the implementation of some WTO Agreements and Decisions, including the difficulties and resource constraints that have been encountered in the implementation of obligations in various areas;

*Recalling* the 3 May 2000 Decision of the General Council to meet in special sessions to address outstanding implementation issues, and to assess the existing difficulties, identify ways needed to resolve them, and take decisions for appropriate action not later than the Fourth Session of the Ministerial Conference;

*Noting* the actions taken by the General Council in pursuance of this mandate at its Special Sessions in October and December 2000 (WT/L/384), as well as the review and further discussion undertaken at the Special Sessions held in April, July and October 2001, including the referral of additional issues to relevant WTO bodies or their chairpersons for further work;

*Noting also* the reports on the issues referred to the General Council from subsidiary bodies and their chairpersons and from the Director-General, and the discussions as well as the clarifications provided and understandings reached on implementation issues in the intensive informal and formal meetings held under this process since May 2000;

*Decides* as follows:

1. <u>General Agreement on Tariffs and Trade 1994 (GATT 1994)</u>

   1.1 Reaffirms that Article XVIII of the GATT 1994 is a special and differential treatment provision for developing countries and that recourse to it should be less onerous than to Article XII of the GATT 1994.

1.2 Noting the issues raised in the report of the Chairperson of the Committee on Market Access (WT/GC/50) concerning the meaning to be given to the phrase “substantial interest” in paragraph 2(d) of Article XIII of the GATT 1994, the Market Access Committee is directed to give further consideration to the issue and make recommendations to the General Council as expeditiously as possible but in any event not later than the end of 2002.

2. Agreement on Agriculture

2.1 Urges Members to exercise restraint in challenging measures notified under the green box by developing countries to promote rural development and adequately address food security concerns.

2.2 Takes note of the report of the Committee on Agriculture (G/AG/11) regarding the implementation of the Decision on Measures Concerning the Possible Negative Effects of the Reform Programme on Least-Developed and Net Food-Importing Developing Countries, and approves the recommendations contained therein regarding (i) food aid; (ii) technical and financial assistance in the context of aid programmes to improve agricultural productivity and infrastructure; (iii) financing normal levels of commercial imports of basic foodstuffs; and (iv) review of follow-up.

2.3 Takes note of the report of the Committee on Agriculture (G/AG/11) regarding the implementation of Article 10.2 of the Agreement on Agriculture, and approves the recommendations and reporting requirements contained therein.

2.4 Takes note of the report of the Committee on Agriculture (G/AG/11) regarding the administration of tariff rate quotas and the submission by Members of addenda to their notifications, and endorses the decision by the Committee to keep this matter under review.

3. Agreement on the Application of Sanitary and Phytosanitary Measures

3.1 Where the appropriate level of sanitary and phytosanitary protection allows scope for the phased introduction of new sanitary and phytosanitary measures, the phrase “longer time-frame for compliance” referred to in Article 10.2 of the Agreement on the Application of Sanitary and Phytosanitary Measures, shall be understood to mean normally a period of not less than 6 months. Where the appropriate level of sanitary and phytosanitary protection does not allow scope for the phased introduction of a new measure, but specific problems are identified by a Member, the Member applying the measure shall upon request enter into consultations with the country with a view to finding a mutually satisfactory solution to the problem while continuing to achieve the importing Member's appropriate level of protection.

3.2 Subject to the conditions specified in paragraph 2 of Annex B to the Agreement on the Application of Sanitary and Phytosanitary Measures, the phrase "reasonable interval" shall be understood to mean normally a period of not less than 6 months. It is understood that timeframes for specific measures have to be considered in the context of the particular circumstances of the measure and actions necessary to implement it. The entry into force of measures which contribute to the liberalization of trade should not be unnecessarily delayed.

3.3 Takes note of the Decision of the Committee on Sanitary and Phytosanitary Measures (G/SPS/19) regarding equivalence, and instructs the Committee to develop expeditiously the specific programme to further the implementation of Article 4 of the Agreement on the Application of Sanitary and Phytosanitary Measures.

3.4 Pursuant to the provisions of Article 12.7 of the Agreement on the Application of Sanitary and Phytosanitary Measures, the Committee on Sanitary and Phytosanitary Measures is instructed to review the operation and implementation of the Agreement on Sanitary and Phytosanitary Measures at least once every four years.

3.5 (i) Takes note of the actions taken to date by the Director-General to facilitate the increased participation of Members at different levels of development in the work of the relevant international standard setting organizations as well as his efforts to coordinate with these organizations and financial institutions in identifying SPS-related technical assistance needs and how best to address them; and

(ii) urges the Director-General to continue his cooperative efforts with these organizations and institutions in this regard, including with a view to according priority to the effective participation of least-developed countries and facilitating the provision of technical and financial assistance for this purpose.

3.6 (i) Urges Members to provide, to the extent possible, the financial and technical assistance necessary to enable least-developed countries to respond adequately to the introduction of any new SPS measures which may have significant negative effects on their trade; and

(ii) urges Members to ensure that technical assistance is provided to least-developed countries with a view to responding to the special problems faced by them in implementing the Agreement on the Application of Sanitary and Phytosanitary Measures.

4. Agreement on Textiles and Clothing

Reaffirms the commitment to full and faithful implementation of the Agreement on Textiles and Clothing, and agrees:

4.1 that the provisions of the Agreement relating to the early integration of products and the elimination of quota restrictions should be effectively utilized.

4.2 that Members will exercise particular consideration before initiating investigations in the context of antidumping remedies on textile and clothing exports from developing countries previously subject to quantitative restrictions under the Agreement for a period of two years following full integration of this Agreement into the WTO.

4.3 that without prejudice to their rights and obligations, Members shall notify any changes in their rules of origin concerning products falling under the coverage of the Agreement to the Committee on Rules of Origin which may decide to examine them.

Requests the Council for Trade in Goods to examine the following proposals:

4.4 that when calculating the quota levels for small suppliers for the remaining years of the Agreement, Members will apply the most favourable methodology available in respect of those Members under the growth-on-growth provisions from the beginning of the implementation period; extend the same treatment to least-developed countries; and, where possible, eliminate quota restrictions on imports of such Members;

4.5 that Members will calculate the quota levels for the remaining years of the Agreement with respect to other restrained Members as if implementation of the growth-on-growth provision for stage 3 had been advanced to 1 January 2000;

and make recommendations to the General Council by 31 July 2002 for appropriate action.

5. Agreement on Technical Barriers to Trade

5.1 Confirms the approach to technical assistance being developed by the Committee on Technical Barriers to Trade, reflecting the results of the triennial review work in this area, and mandates this work to continue.

5.2 Subject to the conditions specified in paragraph 12 of Article 2 of the Agreement on Technical Barriers to Trade, the phrase "reasonable interval" shall be understood to mean normally a period of not less than 6 months, except when this would be ineffective in fulfilling the legitimate objectives pursued.

5.3 (i) Takes note of the actions taken to date by the Director-General to facilitate the increased participation of Members at different levels of development in the work of the relevant international standard setting organizations as well as his efforts to coordinate with these organizations and financial institutions in identifying TBT-related technical assistance needs and how best to address them; and

(ii) urges the Director-General to continue his cooperative efforts with these organizations and institutions, including with a view to according priority to the effective participation of least-developed countries and facilitating the provision of technical and financial assistance for this purpose.

5.4 (i) urges Members to provide, to the extent possible, the financial and technical assistance necessary to enable least-developed countries to respond adequately to the introduction of any new TBT measures which may have significant negative effects on their trade; and

(ii) urges Members to ensure that technical assistance is provided to least-developed countries with a view to responding to the special problems faced by them in implementing the Agreement on Technical Barriers to Trade.

6. Agreement on Trade-Related Investment Measures

6.1 Takes note of the actions taken by the Council for Trade in Goods in regard to requests from some developing-country Members for the extension of the five-year transitional period provided for in Article 5.2 of Agreement on Trade-Related Investment Measures.

6.2 Urges the Council for Trade in Goods to consider positively requests that may be made by least-developed countries under Article 5.3 of the TRIMs Agreement or Article IX.3 of the WTO Agreement, as well as to take into consideration the particular circumstances of least-developed countries when setting the terms and conditions including time-frames.

7. Agreement on the Implementation of Article VI of the General Agreement on Tariffs and Trade 1994

7.1 Agrees that investigating authorities shall examine with special care any application for the initiation of an anti-dumping investigation where an investigation of the same product from the same Member resulted in a negative finding within the 365 days prior to the filing of the application and that, unless this pre-initiation examination indicates that circumstances have changed, the investigation shall not proceed.

7.2 Recognizes that, while Article 15 of the Agreement on the Implementation of Article VI of the General Agreement on Tariffs and Trade 1994 is a mandatory provision, the modalities for its application would benefit from clarification. Accordingly, the Committee on Anti-Dumping Practices is instructed, through its working group on Implementation, to examine this issue and to draw up appropriate recommendations within twelve months on how to operationalize this provision.

7.3 Takes note that Article 5.8 of the Agreement on the Implementation of Article VI of the General Agreement on Tariffs and Trade 1994 does not specify the time-frame to be used in determining the volume of dumped imports, and that this lack of specificity creates uncertainties in the implementation of the provision. The Committee on Anti-Dumping Practices is instructed, through its working group on Implementation, to study this issue and draw up recommendations within 12 months, with a view to ensuring the maximum possible predictability and objectivity in the application of time frames.

7.4 Takes note that Article 18.6 of the Agreement on the Implementation of Article VI of the General Agreement on Tariffs and Trade 1994 requires the Committee on Anti-Dumping Practices to review annually the implementation and operation of the Agreement taking into account the objectives thereof. The Committee on Anti-Dumping Practices is instructed to draw up guidelines for the improvement of annual reviews and to report its views and recommendations to the General Council for subsequent decision within 12 months.

8. Agreement on the Implementation of Article VII of the General Agreement on Tariffs and Trade 1994

8.1 Takes note of the actions taken by the Committee on Customs Valuation in regard to the requests from a number of developing-country Members for the extension of the five-year transitional period provided for in Article 20.1 of Agreement on the Implementation of Article VII of the General Agreement on Tariffs and Trade 1994.

8.2 Urges the Council for Trade in Goods to give positive consideration to requests that may be made by least-developed country Members under paragraphs 1 and 2 of Annex III of the Customs Valuation Agreement or under Article IX.3 of the WTO Agreement, as well as to take into consideration the particular circumstances of least-developed countries when setting the terms and conditions including time-frames.

8.3 Underlines the importance of strengthening cooperation between the customs administrations of Members in the prevention of customs fraud. In this regard, it is agreed that, further to the 1994 Ministerial Decision Regarding Cases Where Customs Administrations Have Reasons to Doubt the Truth or Accuracy of the Declared Value, when the customs administration of an importing Member has reasonable grounds to doubt the truth or accuracy of the declared value, it may seek assistance from the customs administration of an exporting Member on the value of the good concerned. In such cases, the exporting Member shall offer cooperation and assistance, consistent with its domestic laws and procedures, including furnishing information on the export value of the good concerned. Any information provided in this context shall be treated in accordance with Article 10 of the Customs Valuation Agreement. Furthermore, recognizing the legitimate concerns expressed by the customs administrations of several importing Members on the accuracy of the declared value, the Committee on Customs Valuation is directed to identify and assess practical means to address such concerns, including the exchange of information on export values and to report to the General Council by the end of 2002 at the latest.

9. Agreement on Rules of Origin

9.1 Takes note of the report of the Committee on Rules of Origin (G/RO/48) regarding progress on the harmonization work programme, and urges the Committee to complete its work by the end of 2001.

9.2 Agrees that any interim arrangements on rules of origin implemented by Members in the transitional period before the entry into force of the results of the harmonization work programme shall be consistent with the Agreement on Rules of Origin, particularly Articles 2 and 5 thereof. Without prejudice to Members' rights and obligations, such arrangements may be examined by the Committee on Rules of Origin.

10. Agreement on Subsidies and Countervailing Measures

10.1 Agrees that Annex VII(b) to the Agreement on Subsidies and Countervailing Measures includes the Members that are listed therein until their GNP per capita reaches US $1,000 in constant 1990 dollars for three consecutive years. This decision will enter into effect upon the adoption by the Committee on Subsidies and Countervailing Measures of an appropriate methodology for calculating constant 1990 dollars. If, however, the Committee on Subsidies and Countervailing Measures does not reach a consensus agreement on an appropriate methodology by 1 January 2003, the methodology proposed by the Chairman of the Committee set forth in G/SCM/38, Appendix 2 shall be applied. A Member shall not leave Annex VII(b) so long as its GNP per capita in current dollars has not reached US $1,000 based upon the most recent data from the World Bank.

10.2 Takes note of the proposal to treat measures implemented by developing countries with a view to achieving legitimate development goals, such as regional growth, technology research and development funding, production diversification and development and implementation of environmentally sound methods of production as non-actionable subsidies, and agrees that this issue be addressed in accordance with paragraph 13 below. During the course of the negotiations, Members are urged to exercise due restraint with respect to challenging such measures.

10.3 Agrees that the Committee on Subsidies and Countervailing Measures shall continue its review of the provisions of the Agreement on Subsidies and Countervailing Measures regarding countervailing duty investigations and report to the General Council by 31 July 2002.

10.4 Agrees that if a Member has been excluded from the list in paragraph (b) of Annex VII to the Agreement on Subsidies and Countervailing Measures, it shall be re-included in it when its GNP per capita falls back below US$ 1,000.

10.5 Subject to the provisions of Articles 27.5 and 27.6, it is reaffirmed that least-developed country Members are exempt from the prohibition on export subsidies set forth in Article 3.1(a) of the Agreement on Subsidies and Countervailing Measures, and thus have flexibility to finance their exporters, consistent with their development needs. It is understood that the eight-year period in Article 27.5 within which a least-developed country Member must phase out its export subsidies in respect of a product in which it is export-competitive begins from the date export competitiveness exists within the meaning of Article 27.6.

10.6 Having regard to the particular situation of certain developing-country Members, directs the Committee on Subsidies and Countervailing Measures to extend the transition period, under the rubric of Article 27.4 of the Agreement on Subsidies and Countervailing Measures, for certain export subsidies provided by such Members, pursuant to the procedures set forth in document G/SCM/39. Furthermore, when considering a request for an extension of the transition period under the rubric of Article 27.4 of the Agreement on Subsidies and Countervailing Measures, and in order to avoid that Members at similar stages of development and having a similar order of magnitude of share in world trade are treated differently in terms of receiving such extensions for the same eligible programmes and the length of such extensions, directs the Committee to extend the transition period for those developing countries, after taking into account the relative competitiveness in relation to other developing-country

Members who have requested extension of the transition period following the procedures set forth in document G/SCM/39.

11. Agreement on Trade-Related Aspects of Intellectual Property Rights (TRIPS)

11.1 The TRIPS Council is directed to continue its examination of the scope and modalities for complaints of the types provided for under subparagraphs 1(b) and 1(c) of Article XXIII of GATT 1994 and make recommendations to the Fifth Session of the Ministerial Conference. It is agreed that, in the meantime, Members will not initiate such complaints under the TRIPS Agreement.

11.2 Reaffirming that the provisions of Article 66.2 of the TRIPS Agreement are mandatory, it is agreed that the TRIPS Council shall put in place a mechanism for ensuring the monitoring and full implementation of the obligations in question. To this end, developed-country Members shall submit prior to the end of 2002 detailed reports on the functioning in practice of the incentives provided to their enterprises for the transfer of technology in pursuance of their commitments under Article 66.2. These submissions shall be subject to a review in the TRIPS Council and information shall be updated by Members annually.

12. Cross-cutting Issues

12.1 The Committee on Trade and Development is instructed:

(i) to identify those special and differential treatment provisions that are already mandatory in nature and those that are non-binding in character, to consider the legal and practical implications for developed and developing Members of converting special and differential treatment measures into mandatory provisions, to identify those that Members consider should be made mandatory, and to report to the General Council with clear recommendations for a decision by July 2002;

(ii) to examine additional ways in which special and differential treatment provisions can be made more effective, to consider ways, including improved information flows, in which developing countries, in particular the least-developed countries, may be assisted to make best use of special and differential treatment provisions, and to report to the General Council with clear recommendations for a decision by July 2002; and

(iii) to consider, in the context of the work programme adopted at the Fourth Session of the Ministerial Conference, how special and differential treatment may be incorporated into the architecture of WTO rules.

The work of the Committee on Trade and Development in this regard shall take fully into consideration previous work undertaken as noted in WT/COMTD/W/77/Rev.1. It will also be without prejudice to work in respect of implementation of WTO Agreements in the General Council and in other Councils and Committees.

12.2 Reaffirms that preferences granted to developing countries pursuant to the Decision of the Contracting Parties of 28 November 1979 ("Enabling Clause")[1] should be generalized, non-reciprocal and non-discriminatory.

13. Outstanding Implementation Issues[2]

Agrees that outstanding implementation issues be addressed in accordance with paragraph 12 of the Ministerial Declaration (WT/MIN(01)/DEC/1).

14. Final Provisions

Requests the Director-General, consistent with paragraphs 38 to 43 of the Ministerial Declaration (WT/MIN(01)/DEC/1), to ensure that WTO technical assistance focuses, on a priority basis, on assisting developing countries to implement existing WTO obligations as well as on increasing their capacity to participate more effectively in future multilateral trade negotiations. In carrying out this mandate, the WTO Secretariat should cooperate more closely with international and regional intergovernmental organizations so as to increase efficiency and synergies and avoid duplication of programmes.

1 BISD 26S/203.

2 A list of these issues is compiled in document Job(01)/152/Rev.1.

# ANNEX 5

## COMPILATION OF OUTSTANDING IMPLEMENTATION ISSUES RAISED BY MEMBERS REVISION

*JOB(01)/152/Rev.1, 27 October 2001*

This compilation is being circulated by the Secretariat with a view to assisting delegations in their consideration of the outstanding implementation issues. It should be read together with the draft Decision on Implementation-Related Issues and Concerns (Job(01)/139/Rev.1). It lists outstanding implementation issues raised in the draft Ministerial Text of 19 October 1999 (Job(99)/5868/Rev.1) and those subsequently raised by Members during consultations. For ease of reference, the text retains the numbering of the tirets used by the G-7 countries in their paper on implementation.

---

1. General Agreement on Tariffs and Trade 1994

- Tiret 1
  Only the Committee on Balance-of-Payments shall have the authority to examine the overall justification of BOP measures.

- Tiret 3
  A complete review of Article XVIII shall be undertaken with a view to ensure that it subserves the original objective of facilitating the progressive development of economies in developing countries and to allow them to implement programmes and policies of economic development designed to raise the general standard of living of their people.

2. Agreement on Agriculture

- Tiret 6
  If in the calculation of the AMS, domestic support prices are lower than the external reference price (so as to ensure access of poor households to basic foodstuffs), thereby resulting in negative product specific support, then Members shall be allowed to increase their non-product specific support by an equivalent amount.

3. Agreement on the Application of Sanitary and Phytosanitary Measures

Proposal by Brazil, 17 October 2001

- Where the introduction of SPS measures may have significant effect on trade opportunities for products of interest to developing countries, Members shall notify the WTO and inform the concerned Member prior to the application of such measures and, in addition, to the relevant provisions of paragraph 5 of Annex B and Article 7, shall notify final rules or subsequent decisions derived from a previously notified measure.

4. Agreement on Technical Barriers to Trade

- Tiret 33
  Article 11 shall be made obligatory so that technical assistance and cooperation is provided to developing countries.

- Tiret 34
  Acceptance by developed-country importers of self-declaration regarding adherence to standards by developing-country exporters. This provision should be introduced in Article 12.

5. Agreement on Trade-Related Investment Measures

- Tiret 37
  Developing countries shall have another opportunity to notify existing TRIMs measures which they would be then allowed to maintain till the end of the new transition period.

- Tiret 38
  The provisions of Article 5.3 must be suitably amended and made mandatory.

- Tiret 39
  Developing countries shall be exempted from the disciplines on the application of domestic content requirement by providing for an enabling provision in Articles 2 and 4 to this effect.

- Tiret 40
  Specific provisions shall be included in the Agreement to provide developing countries the necessary flexibility to implement development policies (intended to address, among others, social, regional, economic, and technological concerns) that may help reduce the disparities they face *vis-à-vis* developed countries.

6. Agreement on Implementation of Article VI of the GATT 1994

- Tiret 42
  Under Article 9.1 the lesser duty rule shall be made mandatory.

- Tiret 43
  Article 2.2 shall be clarified in order to make appropriate comparison with respect to the margin of dumping.

- Tiret 44
  Provisions of the Agreement shall be improved with a view to prevent the imposition of arbitrary or primarily protectionist measures. The provisions to be revisited should include, *inter alia*, (i) the criteria, methodology, and procedures of the reviews specified in the Agreement (expeditious review for new exporters, final review, reviews upon request), (ii) the definition of the product motivating the investigation, (iii) the determination of the margin of dumping, (iv) the imposition and collection of duties, (v) the "cumulation" clauses.

- Tiret 46
  The existing de minimis dumping margin of 2 per cent of export price below which no anti-dumping duty can be imposed (Article 5.8), needs to be raised to 5 per cent for developing countries.

- Tiret 47
  The proposed de minimis dumping margin of 5 per cent is applied not only in new cases but also in refund and review cases.

- Tiret 48
  The threshold volume of dumped imports which shall normally be regarded as negligible (Article 5.8) should be increased from the existing 3 per cent to [5 per cent] [7 per cent] for imports from developing countries.

- Tiret 50
  The substantial quantities test should be increased from the present threshold of 20 per cent to at least 40 per cent.

- Tiret 51
  Article 2.4.1 shall include details of dealing with foreign exchange rate fluctuations during the process of dumping.

- Tiret 52
  Article 3 shall contain a detailed provision dealing with the determination of the material retardation of the establishment of a domestic industry as stipulated in footnote 9.

- Tiret 53
  There should be a provision in the Agreement, which provides a presumption of dumping of imports from developed countries into developing countries, provided certain conditions are met.

- Tiret 54
  Article 17 should be suitably modified so that the general standard of review laid down in the WTO dispute settlement mechanism applies equally and totally to disputes in the anti-dumping area.

Proposals by Least-Developed Countries, 22 October 2001

- The General Council agrees that simplified procedures for taking anti-dumping action shall be devised for the use of LDCs.

- The General Council agrees that the threshold for volume of imports referred to in Article 5.8 of the Agreement shall be increased from 3 percent to 7 percent in the case of LDCs. LDCs shall be exempted from cumulation.

7. Agreement on Implementation of Article VII of GATT 1994

- Tiret 57
  The addition of cost of services such as engineering, development, and design work, which are supplied directly or indirectly by the buyer free of charge or at reduced cost for the production of goods under import, shall be included in Article 8:1(b)(iv).

- Tiret 58
  The residual method of determining customs value under Article 7 shall be inclusive of all residual eventualities, thus allowing valuation based on domestic market price or export price in a third country with appropriate adjustments.

- Tiret 59
  The Agreement should be amended to provide for the highest value when more than one transaction value of identical or similar goods is found.

- Tiret 60
  Buying commissions should be taken into account in the determination of customs value of imported goods as it forms a legitimate component of the landed cost of imported goods.

- Tiret 61
  Persons associated with each other as sole agents, sole distributors, and sole concessionaires, howsoever described, should automatically be deemed "related".

8. Agreement on Subsidies and Countervailing Measures

- Tiret 64
  Article 8:1 of the Subsidies Agreement dealing with non-actionable subsidies shall be expanded to include subsidies referred to in Article 3:1 of the Agreement when such subsidies are provided by developing country Members.

- Tiret 65
  Export credits given by developing countries shall not be considered as subsidies so long as the rates at which they are extended are above LIBOR.

- Tiret 66
  Any countervailing duties shall be restricted only to that amount by which the subsidy exceeds the de minimis level.

- Tiret 67
  Annex VII of the Agreement shall be modified to read as follows:
  The developing-country Members not subject to the provisions of paragraph 1(a) of Article 3 under the terms of paragraph 2(a) of Article 27 are:
  (i) The developing countries, including the least-developed countries, Members of the WTO that are included in the Low and Middle Income Category of the World Bank;
  (ii) Countries indicated in paragraph (i) above will be excluded from this Annex if their GNP per capita has exceeded the top level of the Middle Income Category of the World Bank. They will be automatically included in this Annex, if their GNP per capita falls at or under the top level of the Lower-Middle Income Category of the World Bank.

- Tiret 68
  The prohibition on using export subsidies under Article 27:6 shall be applicable to a developing country only after its export levels in a product have remained over 3.25 per cent of world trade continuously for a period of five years.

- Tiret 70
  Article 27.2 shall be amended so that the Article 3.1(a) prohibition does not apply to export subsidies granted by developing countries where they account for less than 5 per cent of the f.o.b. value of the product.

- Tiret 71
  Countervailing measures shall not be imposed in the case of imports from developing countries where the total volume of imports is negligible, i.e. 7 per cent of total imports.

- Tiret 72
  Aggregate and generalized rates of duty rate remission should be allowed in case of developing countries even though the individual units may not be able to establish the source of their inputs.

- Tiret 73
  Developing countries should be allowed to neutralize the cost escalating effect of taxes.

- Tiret 74
  Article 11:9 should be modified to provide an additional dispensation for developing countries, in as much as that any subsidy investigation shall be immediately terminated in cases where the subsidy being provided by a

developing country is less than 2.5 per cent *ad valorem*, instead of the existing de minimis of 1 per cent presently applicable to all Members.

- Tiret 75
  The present de minimis level of 3 per cent below which countervailing duties may not be imposed for developing countries, needs to be increased (Article 27:11).

- Tiret 76
  There should be a clarification in Article 27:3 that it is applicable notwithstanding the provisions of any other agreement.

- Tiret 77
  The definition of "inputs consumed in the production process" (footnote 61) needs to be expanded to include all inputs, not just physical inputs, which may have contributed to the determination of the final cost price of the exported product.

- Tiret 78
  Annex I of the Agreement shall be amended to provide developing countries the flexibility to finance their exporters, consistent with their developmental objectives.

- Tiret 79
  The provisions of Article 27 shall be re-evaluated so as to address, under a permanent and more adequate framework, the needs and specificities of developing countries concerning incentives and subsidies.

- Tiret 81
  The language of Annex I of the Agreement, particularly item 'k', shall be reviewed to permit developing countries to provide competitive export financing *vis-à-vis* the conditions found in the international market or those offered by the credit agencies of developed countries (controlled by and or acting under the authorities of the governments).

- Tiret 83
  The SCM Committee shall review the threshold of US$ 1000 in Annex VII (b) and examine the possibility of including in Annex VII, Members in the low and lower-middle income categories as classified by the World Bank. The SCM Committee shall examine additional possibilities for granting flexibility to developing countries such as threshold limits relating to percentage share of exports in import markets and in global trade.

Proposals by Least-Developed Countries, 22 October 2001

- The General Council agrees that subsidies required for development, diversification and upgrading infant industries including freight rebate schemes in developing countries shall be treated as non-actionable subsidy.

- The General Council agrees that LDCs shall be exempted from competitiveness thresholds of subsidies and the threshold for imports referred to Article 27.10 of the Agreement shall be increased from 4 per cent to 10 per cent in case of LDCs. LDCs shall be exempted from cumulation.

- The General Council agrees that financial resources shall be provided to LDCs to enable them to meet their special needs, in particular with respect to subsidies covered by Article 8.2 (c) (green subsidies).

9. <u>Agreement on Safeguards</u>

- Tiret 84
  Article 9.1 shall be amended so that safeguard measures are not applied to imports from developing countries which individually account for less than 7 per cent of total imports and 15 per cent collectively.

10. <u>Agreement on Trade-Related Aspects of Intellectual Property Rights</u>

- Tiret 87
  In the light of provisions contained in Articles 23 and 24 of the TRIPS Agreement, additional protection for geographical indications shall be extended for products other than wines and spirits.

- Tiret 88
  A clear understanding in the interim that patents inconsistent with Article 15 of the CBD shall not be granted.

- Tiret 91
  The period given for implementation of the provisions of Article 27.3(b) shall be five years from the date the review is completed.

- Tiret 93
  The transitional period for developing countries provided for in Article 65.2 shall be extended.

Proposal by Least-Developed Countries, 22 October 2001

- The General Council agrees that the transition period for LDCs shall be extended so long as they retain the status of an LDC.

- Tiret 94
  Articles 7 and 8 of the TRIPS Agreement to be operationalized by providing for transfer of technology on fair and mutually advantageous terms.

- Tiret 95
  [Article 27.3(b) to be amended in light of the provisions of the Convention on Biological Diversity and the International Undertaking. Also, clarify artificial

distinctions between biological and microbiological organisms and process; ensure the continuation of the traditional farming practices including the right to save, exchange and save seeds, and sell their harvest; and prevent anti-competitive practices which will threaten food sovereignty of people in developing countries, as permitted by Article 31 of the TRIPS Agreement.] [Article 27.3(b) should be amended to take into account the Convention on Biological Diversity and the International Undertaking on Plant Genetic Resources. The amendments should clarify and satisfactorily resolve the analytical distinctions between biological and microbiological organisms and processed; that all living organisms and their parts cannot be patented; and those natural processes that produce living organisms should not be patentable. The amendments should ensure the protection of innovations of indigenous and local farming communities; the continuation of traditional farming processes including the right to use, exchange and save seeds, and promote food security.]

Proposal by Least-Developed Countries, 22 October 2001

- The General Council agrees that the review process should clarify that all living organisms, including plants, animals and parts of plants and animals, including gene sequences, and biological and other natural processes for the production of plants, animals and their parts, shall not be granted patents.

11. Cross-cutting issues

- Tiret 98

  Having regard to the significant role played by preferential trading agreements between developing and developed countries, Members agree to consider favourably, as appropriate, the granting or extension of waivers to Article I of GATT 1994 covering such agreements.

- Tiret 99

  The General Council shall adopt measures designed to secure a redistribution of negotiating rights in favour of small and medium-sized exporting Members in trade negotiations.

# ANNEX 6

## DECLARATION ON THE TRIPS AGREEMENT AND PUBLIC HEALTH

*Adopted by the Doha Ministerial Conference on 14 November 2001*

1. We recognize the gravity of the public health problems afflicting many developing and least-developed countries, especially those resulting from HIV/AIDS, tuberculosis, malaria and other epidemics.

2. We stress the need for the WTO Agreement on Trade-Related Aspects of Intellectual Property Rights (TRIPS Agreement) to be part of the wider national and international action to address these problems.

3. We recognize that intellectual property protection is important for the development of new medicines. We also recognize the concerns about its effects on prices.

4. We agree that the TRIPS Agreement does not and should not prevent Members from taking measures to protect public health. Accordingly, while reiterating our commitment to the TRIPS Agreement, we affirm that the Agreement can and should be interpreted and implemented in a manner supportive of WTO Members' right to protect public health and, in particular, to promote access to medicines for all.

   In this connection, we reaffirm the right of WTO Members to use, to the full, the provisions in the TRIPS Agreement, which provide flexibility for this purpose.

5. Accordingly and in the light of paragraph 4 above, while maintaining our commitments in the TRIPS Agreement, we recognize that these flexibilities include:

   (a) In applying the customary rules of interpretation of public international law, each provision of the TRIPS Agreement shall be read in the light of the object and purpose of the Agreement as expressed, in particular, in its objectives and principles.
   (b) Each Member has the right to grant compulsory licences and the freedom to determine the grounds upon which such licences are granted.
   (c) Each Member has the right to determine what constitutes a national emergency or other circumstances of extreme urgency, it being understood that public health crises, including those relating to HIV/AIDS, tuberculosis, malaria and other epidemics, can represent a national emergency or other circumstances of extreme urgency.
   (d) The effect of the provisions in the TRIPS Agreement that are relevant to the exhaustion of intellectual property rights is to leave each Member free to

establish its own regime for such exhaustion without challenge, subject to the MFN and national treatment provisions of Articles 3 and 4.

6. We recognize that WTO Members with insufficient or no manufacturing capacities in the pharmaceutical sector could face difficulties in making effective use of compulsory licensing under the TRIPS Agreement. We instruct the Council for TRIPS to find an expeditious solution to this problem and to report to the General Council before the end of 2002.

7. We reaffirm the commitment of developed-country Members to provide incentives to their enterprises and institutions to promote and encourage technology transfer to least-developed country Members pursuant to Article 66.2. We also agree that the least-developed country Members will not be obliged, with respect to pharmaceutical products, to implement or apply Sections 5 and 7 of Part II of the TRIPS Agreement or to enforce rights provided for under these Sections until 1 January 2016, without prejudice to the right of least-developed country Members to seek other extensions of the transition periods as provided for in Article 66.1 of the TRIPS Agreement. We instruct the Council for TRIPS to take the necessary action to give effect to this pursuant to Article 66.1 of the TRIPS Agreement.

# ANNEX 7

## IMPLEMENTATION OF PARAGRAPH 6 OF THE DOHA DECLARATION ON THE TRIPS AGREEMENT AND PUBLIC HEALTH

*General Council Decision of 30 August 2003**

The General Council,

*Having regard* to paragraphs 1, 3 and 4 of Article IX of the Marrakesh Agreement Establishing the World Trade Organization ("the WTO Agreement");

*Conducting* the functions of the Ministerial Conference in the interval between meetings pursuant to paragraph 2 of Article IV of the WTO Agreement;

*Noting* the Declaration on the TRIPS Agreement and Public Health (WT/MIN(01)/DEC/2) (the "Declaration") and, in particular, the instruction of the Ministerial Conference to the Council for TRIPS contained in paragraph 6 of the Declaration to find an expeditious solution to the problem of the difficulties that WTO Members with insufficient or no manufacturing capacities in the pharmaceutical sector could face in making effective use of compulsory licensing under the TRIPS Agreement and to report to the General Council before the end of 2002;

*Recognizing,* where eligible importing Members seek to obtain supplies under the system set out in this Decision, the importance of a rapid response to those needs consistent with the provisions of this Decision;

*Noting* that, in the light of the foregoing, exceptional circumstances exist justifying waivers from the obligations set out in paragraphs (f) and (h) of Article 31 of the TRIPS Agreement with respect to pharmaceutical products;

*Decides* as follows:

1. For the purposes of this Decision:

   (a) "pharmaceutical product" means any patented product, or product manufactured through a patented process, of the pharmaceutical sector needed to address the public health problems as recognized in paragraph 1 of the Declaration. It is understood that active ingredients necessary for its manufacture and diagnostic kits needed for its use would be included[1];

   (b) "eligible importing Member" means any least-developed country Member, and any other Member that has made a notification[2] to the Council for TRIPS of its intention to use the system as an importer, it being understood that a Member may notify at any time that it will use the system in whole or in a limited way, for example only in the case of a national emergency or other circumstances of extreme urgency or in cases of public non-commercial use. It is noted that some Members will not use the system set out in this Decision as importing Members[3] and that some other Members have stated that, if they use the system, it would be in no more than situations of national emergency or other circumstances of extreme urgency;

(c) "exporting Member" means a Member using the system set out in this Decision to produce pharmaceutical products for, and export them to, an eligible importing Member.

2. The obligations of an exporting Member under Article 31(f) of the TRIPS Agreement shall be waived with respect to the grant by it of a compulsory licence to the extent necessary for the purposes of production of a pharmaceutical product(s) and its export to an eligible importing Member(s) in accordance with the terms set out below in this paragraph:

(a) the eligible importing Member(s)[4] has made a notification[2] to the Council for TRIPS, that:
(i) specifies the names and expected quantities of the product(s) needed[5];
(ii) confirms that the eligible importing Member in question, other than a least-developed country Member, has established that it has insufficient or no manufacturing capacities in the pharmaceutical sector for the product(s) in question in one of the ways set out in the Annex to this Decision; and
(iii) confirms that, where a pharmaceutical product is patented in its territory, it has granted or intends to grant a compulsory licence in accordance with Article 31 of the TRIPS Agreement and the provisions of this Decision[6];

(b) the compulsory licence issued by the exporting Member under this Decision shall contain the following conditions:
(i) only the amount necessary to meet the needs of the eligible importing Member(s) may be manufactured under the licence and the entirety of this production shall be exported to the Member(s) which has notified its needs to the Council for TRIPS;
(ii) products produced under the licence shall be clearly identified as being produced under the system set out in this Decision through specific labelling or marking. Suppliers should distinguish such products through special packaging and/or special colouring/shaping of the products themselves, provided that such distinction is feasible and does not have a significant impact on price; and
(iii) before shipment begins, the licensee shall post on a website[7] the following information:

- the quantities being supplied to each destination as referred to in indent (i) above; and
- the distinguishing features of the product(s) referred to in indent (ii) above;

(c) the exporting Member shall notify[8] the Council for TRIPS of the grant of the licence, including the conditions attached to it.[9] The information provided shall include the name and address of the licensee, the product(s) for which the licence has been granted, the quantity(ies) for which it has been granted, the country(ies) to which the product(s) is (are) to be supplied and the duration of the licence. The notification shall also indicate the address of the website referred to in subparagraph (b)(iii) above.

3. Where a compulsory licence is granted by an exporting Member under the system set out in this Decision, adequate remuneration pursuant to Article 31(h) of the TRIPS Agreement shall be paid in that Member taking into account the economic value to the importing Member of the use that has been authorized in the exporting Member. Where a compulsory licence is granted for the same products in the eligible importing Member, the obligation of that Member under Article 31(h) shall be waived in respect of those products for which remuneration in accordance with the first sentence of this paragraph is paid in the exporting Member.

4. In order to ensure that the products imported under the system set out in this Decision are used for the public health purposes underlying their importation, eligible importing Members shall take reasonable measures within their means, proportionate to their administrative capacities and to the risk of trade diversion to prevent re-exportation of the products that have actually been imported into their territories under the system. In the event that an eligible importing Member that is a developing country Member or a least-developed country Member experiences difficulty in implementing this provision, developed country Members shall provide, on request and on mutually agreed terms and conditions, technical and financial cooperation in order to facilitate its implementation.

5. Members shall ensure the availability of effective legal means to prevent the importation into, and sale in, their territories of products produced under the system set out in this Decision and diverted to their markets inconsistently with its provisions, using the means already required to be available under the TRIPS Agreement. If any Member considers that such measures are proving insufficient for this purpose, the matter may be reviewed in the Council for TRIPS at the request of that Member.

6. With a view to harnessing economies of scale for the purposes of enhancing purchasing power for, and facilitating the local production of, pharmaceutical products:

(i) where a developing or least-developed country WTO Member is a party to a regional trade agreement within the meaning of Article XXIV of the GATT 1994 and the Decision of 28 November 1979 on Differential and

More Favourable Treatment Reciprocity and Fuller Participation of Developing Countries (L/4903), at least half of the current membership of which is made up of countries presently on the United Nations list of least-developed countries, the obligation of that Member under Article 31(f) of the TRIPS Agreement shall be waived to the extent necessary to enable a pharmaceutical product produced or imported under a compulsory licence in that Member to be exported to the markets of those other developing or least-developed country parties to the regional trade agreement that share the health problem in question. It is understood that this will not prejudice the territorial nature of the patent rights in question;

(ii) it is recognized that the development of systems providing for the grant of regional patents to be applicable in the above Members should be promoted. To this end, developed country Members undertake to provide technical cooperation in accordance with Article 67 of the TRIPS Agreement, including in conjunction with other relevant intergovernmental organizations.

7. Members recognize the desirability of promoting the transfer of technology and capacity building in the pharmaceutical sector in order to overcome the problem identified in paragraph 6 of the Declaration. To this end, eligible importing Members and exporting Members are encouraged to use the system set out in this Decision in a way which would promote this objective. Members undertake to cooperate in paying special attention to the transfer of technology and capacity building in the pharmaceutical sector in the work to be undertaken pursuant to Article 66.2 of the TRIPS Agreement, paragraph 7 of the Declaration and any other relevant work of the Council for TRIPS.

8. The Council for TRIPS shall review annually the functioning of the system set out in this Decision with a view to ensuring its effective operation and shall annually report on its operation to the General Council. This review shall be deemed to fulfil the review requirements of Article IX:4 of the WTO Agreement.

9. This Decision is without prejudice to the rights, obligations and flexibilities that Members have under the provisions of the TRIPS Agreement other than paragraphs (f) and (h) of Article 31, including those reaffirmed by the Declaration, and to their interpretation. It is also without prejudice to the extent to which pharmaceutical products produced under a compulsory licence can be exported under the present provisions of Article 31(f) of the TRIPS Agreement.

10. Members shall not challenge any measures taken in conformity with the provisions of the waivers contained in this Decision under subparagraphs 1(b) and 1(c) of Article XXIII of GATT 1994.

11. This Decision, including the waivers granted in it, shall terminate for each Member on the date on which an amendment to the TRIPS Agreement replacing its provisions

takes effect for that Member. The TRIPS Council shall initiate by the end of 2003 work on the preparation of such an amendment with a view to its adoption within six months, on the understanding that the amendment will be based, where appropriate, on this Decision and on the further understanding that it will not be part of the negotiations referred to in paragraph 45 of the Doha Ministerial Declaration (WT/MIN(01)/DEC/1).

## ANNEX

### Assessment of Manufacturing Capacities in the Pharmaceutical Sector

Least-developed country Members are deemed to have insufficient or no manufacturing capacities in the pharmaceutical sector.

For other eligible importing Members insufficient or no manufacturing capacities for the product(s) in question may be established in either of the following ways:

(i) the Member in question has established that it has no manufacturing capacity in the pharmaceutical sector;

**OR**

(ii) where the Member has some manufacturing capacity in this sector, it has examined this capacity and found that, excluding any capacity owned or controlled by the patent owner, it is currently insufficient for the purposes of meeting its needs. When it is established that such capacity has become sufficient to meet the Member's needs, the system shall no longer apply.

---

* This Decision was adopted by the General Council in the light of a statement read out by the Chairman, which can be found in JOB(03)/177. This statement will be reproduced in the minutes of the General Council to be issued as WT/GC/M/82.

1 This subparagraph is without prejudice to subparagraph 1(b).

2 It is understood that this notification does not need to be approved by a WTO body in order to use the system set out in this Decision.

3 Australia, Austria, Belgium, Canada, Denmark, Finland, France, Germany, Greece, Iceland, Ireland, Italy, Japan, Luxembourg, the Netherlands, New Zealand, Norway, Portugal, Spain, Sweden, Switzerland, the United Kingdom and the United States.

4 Joint notifications providing the information required under this subparagraph may be made by the regional organizations referred to in paragraph 6 of this Decision on behalf of eligible importing Members using the system that are parties to them, with the agreement of those parties.

5 The notification will be made available publicly by the WTO Secretariat through a page on the WTO website dedicated to this Decision.

6 This subparagraph is without prejudice to Article 66.1 of the TRIPS Agreement.

7 The licensee may use for this purpose its own website or, with the assistance of the WTO Secretariat, the page on the WTO website dedicated to this Decision.

8 It is understood that this notification does not need to be approved by a WTO body in order to use the system set out in this Decision.

9 The notification will be made available publicly by the WTO Secretariat through a page on the WTO website dedicated to this Decision.

## ANNEX 8

## SELECTED EXCERPTS FROM THE HONG KONG MINISTERIAL DECLARATION

*The Declaration was adopted by the Hong Kong Ministerial Conference on 18 December 2005*

**Agriculture negotiations**

4. We reaffirm our commitment to the mandate on agriculture as set out in paragraph 13 of the Doha Ministerial Declaration and to the Framework adopted by the General Council on 1 August 2004. We take note of the report by the Chairman of the Special Session on his own responsibility (TN/AG/21, contained in Annex A). We welcome the progress made by the Special Session of the Committee on Agriculture since 2004 and recorded therein.

5. On domestic support, there will be three bands for reductions in Final Bound Total AMS and in the overall cut in trade-distorting domestic support, with higher linear cuts in higher bands. In both cases, the Member with the highest level of permitted support will be in the top band, the two Members with the second and third highest levels of support will be in the middle band and all other Members, including all developing country Members, will be in the bottom band. In addition, developed country Members in the lower bands with high relative levels of Final Bound Total AMS will make an additional effort in AMS reduction. We also note that there has been some convergence concerning the reductions in Final Bound Total AMS, the overall cut in trade-distorting domestic support and in both product-specific and non product-specific *de minimis* limits. Disciplines will be developed to achieve effective cuts in trade-distorting domestic support consistent with the Framework. The overall reduction in trade-distorting domestic support will still need to be made even if the sum of the reductions in Final Bound Total AMS, *de minimis* and Blue Box payments would otherwise be less than that overall reduction. Developing country Members with no AMS commitments will be exempt from reductions in *de minimis* and the overall cut in trade-distorting domestic support. Green Box criteria will be reviewed in line with paragraph 16 of the Framework, *inter alia*, to ensure that programmes of developing country Members that cause not more than minimal trade-distortion are effectively covered.

6. We agree to ensure the parallel elimination of all forms of export subsidies and disciplines on all export measures with equivalent effect to be completed by the end of 2013. This will be achieved in a progressive and parallel manner, to be specified in the modalities, so that a substantial part is realized by the end of the first half of the implementation period. We note emerging convergence on some elements of disciplines with respect to export credits, export credit guarantees or insurance

programmes with repayment periods of 180 days and below. We agree that such programmes should be self-financing, reflecting market consistency, and that the period should be of a sufficiently short duration so as not to effectively circumvent real commercially-oriented discipline. As a means of ensuring that trade-distorting practices of STEs are eliminated, disciplines relating to exporting STEs will extend to the future use of monopoly powers so that such powers cannot be exercised in any way that would circumvent the direct disciplines on STEs on export subsidies, government financing and the underwriting of losses. On food aid, we reconfirm our commitment to maintain an adequate level and to take into account the interests of food aid recipient countries. To this end, a "safe box" for bona fide food aid will be provided to ensure that there is no unintended impediment to dealing with emergency situations. Beyond that, we will ensure elimination of commercial displacement. To this end, we will agree effective disciplines on in-kind food aid, monetization and re-exports so that there can be no loop-hole for continuing export subsidization. The disciplines on export credits, export credit guarantees or insurance programmes, exporting state trading enterprises and food aid will be completed by 30 April 2006 as part of the modalities, including appropriate provision in favour of least-developed and net food-importing developing countries as provided for in paragraph 4 of the Marrakesh Decision. The date above for the elimination of all forms of export subsidies, together with the agreed progressivity and parallelism, will be confirmed only upon the completion of the modalities. Developing country Members will continue to benefit from the provisions of Article 9.4 of the Agreement on Agriculture for five years after the end-date for elimination of all forms of export subsidies.

7. On market access, we note the progress made on *ad valorem* equivalents. We adopt four bands for structuring tariff cuts, recognizing that we need now to agree on the relevant thresholds – including those applicable for developing country Members. We recognize the need to agree on treatment of sensitive products, taking into account all the elements involved. We also note that there have been some recent movements on the designation and treatment of Special Products and elements of the Special Safeguard Mechanism. Developing country Members will have the flexibility to self-designate an appropriate number of tariff lines as Special Products guided by indicators based on the criteria of food security, livelihood security and rural development. Developing country Members will also have the right to have recourse to a Special Safeguard Mechanism based on import quantity and price triggers, with precise arrangements to be further defined. Special Products and the Special Safeguard Mechanism shall be an integral part of the modalities and the outcome of negotiations in agriculture.

8. On other elements of special and differential treatment, we note in particular the consensus that exists in the Framework on several issues in all three pillars of domestic support, export competition and market access and that some progress has been made on other special and differential treatment issues.

9. We reaffirm that nothing we have agreed here compromises the agreement already reflected in the Framework on other issues including tropical products and products

of particular importance to the diversification of production from the growing of illicit narcotic crops, long-standing preferences and preference erosion.

10. However, we recognize that much remains to be done in order to establish modalities and to conclude the negotiations. Therefore, we agree to intensify work on all outstanding issues to fulfil the Doha objectives, in particular, we are resolved to establish modalities no later than 30 April 2006 and to submit comprehensive draft Schedules based on these modalities no later than 31 July 2006.

**Cotton**

11. We recall the mandate given by the Members in the Decision adopted by the General Council on 1 August 2004 to address cotton ambitiously, expeditiously and specifically, within the agriculture negotiations in relation to all trade-distorting policies affecting the sector in all three pillars of market access, domestic support and export competition, as specified in the Doha text and the July 2004 Framework text. We note the work already undertaken in the Sub-Committee on Cotton and the proposals made with regard to this matter. Without prejudice to Members' current WTO rights and obligations, including those flowing from actions taken by the Dispute Settlement Body, we reaffirm our commitment to ensure having an explicit decision on cotton within the agriculture negotiations and through the Sub-Committee on Cotton ambitiously, expeditiously and specifically as follows:

– All forms of export subsidies for cotton will be eliminated by developed countries in 2006.

– On market access, developed countries will give duty and quota free access for cotton exports from least-developed countries (LDCs) from the commencement of the implementation period.

– Members agree that the objective is that, as an outcome for the negotiations, trade distorting domestic subsidies for cotton production be reduced more ambitiously than under whatever general formula is agreed and that it should be implemented over a shorter period of time than generally applicable. We commit ourselves to give priority in the negotiations to reach such an outcome.

12. With regard to the development assistance aspects of cotton, we welcome the Consultative Framework process initiated by the Director-General to implement the decisions on these aspects pursuant to paragraph 1.b of the Decision adopted by the General Council on 1 August 2004. We take note of his Periodic Reports and the positive evolution of development assistance noted therein. We urge the Director-General to further intensify his consultative efforts with bilateral donors and with multilateral and regional institutions, with emphasis on improved coherence, coordination and enhanced implementation and to explore the possibility of establishing through such institutions a mechanism to deal with income declines in

the cotton sector until the end of subsidies. Noting the importance of achieving enhanced efficiency and competitiveness in the cotton producing process, we urge the development community to further scale up its cotton-specific assistance and to support the efforts of the Director-General. In this context, we urge Members to promote and support South-South cooperation, including transfer of technology. We welcome the domestic reform efforts by African cotton producers aimed at enhancing productivity and efficiency, and encourage them to deepen this process. We reaffirm the complementarity of the trade policy and development assistance aspects of cotton. We invite the Director-General to furnish a third Periodic Report to our next Session with updates, at appropriate intervals in the meantime, to the General Council, while keeping the Sub-Committee on Cotton fully informed of progress. Finally, as regards follow up and monitoring, we request the Director-General to set up an appropriate follow-up and monitoring mechanism.

**NAMA negotiations**

13. We reaffirm our commitment to the mandate for negotiations on market access for non-agricultural products as set out in paragraph 16 of the Doha Ministerial Declaration. We also reaffirm all the elements of the NAMA Framework adopted by the General Council on 1 August 2004. We take note of the report by the Chairman of the Negotiating Group on Market Access on his own responsibility (TN/MA/16, contained in Annex B). We welcome the progress made by the Negotiating Group on Market Access since 2004 and recorded therein.

14. We adopt a Swiss Formula with coefficients at levels which shall *inter alia*:

– Reduce or as appropriate eliminate tariffs, including the reduction or elimination of tariff peaks, high tariffs and tariff escalation, in particular on products of export interest to developing countries; and

– Take fully into account the special needs and interests of developing countries, including through less than full reciprocity in reduction commitments.

We instruct the Negotiating Group to finalize its structure and details as soon as possible.

15. We reaffirm the importance of special and differential treatment and less than full reciprocity in reduction commitments, including paragraph 8 of the NAMA Framework, as integral parts of the modalities. We instruct the Negotiating Group to finalize its details as soon as possible.

16. In furtherance of paragraph 7 of the NAMA Framework, we recognize that Members are pursuing sectoral initiatives. To this end, we instruct the Negotiating Group to review proposals with a view to identifying those which could garner sufficient participation to be realized. Participation should be on a non-mandatory basis.

17. For the purpose of the second indent of paragraph 5 of the NAMA Framework, we adopt a non-linear mark-up approach to establish base rates for commencing tariff reductions. We instruct the Negotiating Group to finalize its details as soon as possible.

18. We take note of the progress made to convert non *ad valorem* duties to *ad valorem* equivalents on the basis of an agreed methodology as contained in JOB(05)/166/ Rev.1.

19. We take note of the level of common understanding reached on the issue of product coverage and direct the Negotiating Group to resolve differences on the limited issues that remain as quickly as possible.

20. As a supplement to paragraph 16 of the NAMA Framework, we recognize the challenges that may be faced by non-reciprocal preference beneficiary Members as a consequence of the MFN liberalization that will result from these negotiations. We instruct the Negotiating Group to intensify work on the assessment of the scope of the problem with a view to finding possible solutions.

21. We note the concerns raised by small, vulnerable economies, and instruct the Negotiating Group to establish ways to provide flexibilities for these Members without creating a sub-category of WTO Members.

22. We note that the Negotiating Group has made progress in the identification, categorization and examination of notified NTBs. We also take note that Members are developing bilateral, vertical and horizontal approaches to the NTB negotiations, and that some of the NTBs are being addressed in other fora including other Negotiating Groups. We recognize the need for specific negotiating proposals and encourage participants to make such submissions as quickly as possible.

23. However, we recognize that much remains to be done in order to establish modalities and to conclude the negotiations. Therefore, we agree to intensify work on all outstanding issues to fulfil the Doha objectives, in particular, we are resolved to establish modalities no later than 30 April 2006 and to submit comprehensive draft Schedules based on these modalities no later than 31 July 2006.

**Balance between Agriculture and NAMA**

24. We recognize that it is important to advance the development objectives of this Round through enhanced market access for developing countries in both Agriculture and NAMA. To that end, we instruct our negotiators to ensure that there is a comparably high level of ambition in market access for Agriculture and NAMA. This ambition is to be achieved in a balanced and proportionate manner consistent with the principle of special and differential treatment.

## Services negotiations

25. The negotiations on trade in services shall proceed to their conclusion with a view to promoting the economic growth of all trading partners and the development of developing and least-developed countries, and with due respect for the right of Members to regulate. In this regard, we recall and reaffirm the objectives and principles stipulated in the GATS, the Doha Ministerial Declaration, the Guidelines and Procedures for the Negotiations on Trade in Services adopted by the Special Session of the Council for Trade in Services on 28 March 2001 and the Modalities for the Special Treatment for Least-Developed Country Members in the Negotiations on Trade in Services adopted on 3 September 2003, as well as Annex C of the Decision adopted by the General Council on 1 August 2004.

26. We urge all Members to participate actively in these negotiations towards achieving a progressively higher level of liberalization of trade in services, with appropriate flexibility for individual developing countries as provided for in Article XIX of the GATS. Negotiations shall have regard to the size of economies of individual Members, both overall and in individual sectors. We recognize the particular economic situation of LDCs, including the difficulties they face, and acknowledge that they are not expected to undertake new commitments.

27. We are determined to intensify the negotiations in accordance with the above principles and the Objectives, Approaches and Timelines set out in Annex C to this document with a view to expanding the sectoral and modal coverage of commitments and improving their quality. In this regard, particular attention will be given to sectors and modes of supply of export interest to developing countries.

---

## ANNEX C

## SERVICES

### Objectives

1. In order to achieve a progressively higher level of liberalization of trade in services, with appropriate flexibility for individual developing country Members, we agree that Members should be guided, to the maximum extent possible, by the following objectives in making their new and improved commitments:

   (a) Mode 1

      (i) commitments at existing levels of market access on a non-discriminatory basis across sectors of interest to Members

      (ii) removal of existing requirements of commercial presence

(b) Mode 2

(i) commitments at existing levels of market access on a non-discriminatory basis across sectors of interest to Members

(ii) commitments on mode 2 where commitments on mode 1 exist

(c) Mode 3

(i) commitments on enhanced levels of foreign equity participation

(ii) removal or substantial reduction of economic needs tests

(iii) commitments allowing greater flexibility on the types of legal entity permitted

(d) Mode 4

(i) new or improved commitments on the categories of Contractual Services Suppliers, Independent Professionals and Others, de-linked from commercial presence, to reflect *inter alia*:

– removal or substantial reduction of economic needs tests

– indication of prescribed duration of stay and possibility of renewal, if any

(ii) new or improved commitments on the categories of Intra-corporate Transferees and Business Visitors, to reflect *inter alia*:

– removal or substantial reduction of economic needs tests

– indication of prescribed duration of stay and possibility of renewal, if any

(e) MFN Exemptions

(i) removal or substantial reduction of exemptions from most-favoured-nation (MFN) treatment

(ii) clarification of remaining MFN exemptions in terms of scope of application and duration

(f) Scheduling of Commitments

(i) ensuring clarity, certainty, comparability and coherence in the scheduling and classification of commitments through adherence to, *inter alia*, the Scheduling Guidelines pursuant to the Decision of the Council for Trade in Services adopted on 23 March 2001

(ii) ensuring that scheduling of any remaining economic needs tests adheres to the Scheduling Guidelines pursuant to the Decision of the Council for Trade in Services adopted on 23 March 2001.

2. As a reference for the request-offer negotiations, the sectoral and modal objectives as identified by Members may be considered.[1]

3. Members shall pursue full and effective implementation of the Modalities for the Special Treatment for Least-Developed Country Members in the Negotiations on Trade in Services (LDC Modalities) adopted by the Special Session of the Council for Trade in Services on 3 September 2003, with a view to the beneficial and meaningful integration of LDCs into the multilateral trading system.

4. Members must intensify their efforts to conclude the negotiations on rule-making under GATS Articles X, XIII, and XV in accordance with their respective mandates and timelines:

(a) Members should engage in more focused discussions in connection with the technical and procedural questions relating to the operation and application of any possible emergency safeguard measures in services.

(b) On government procurement, Members should engage in more focused discussions and in this context put greater emphasis on proposals by Members, in accordance with Article XIII of the GATS.

(c) On subsidies, Members should intensify their efforts to expedite and fulfil the information exchange required for the purpose of such negotiations, and should engage in more focused discussions on proposals by Members, including the development of a possible working definition of subsidies in services.

5. Members shall develop disciplines on domestic regulation pursuant to the mandate under Article VI:4 of the GATS before the end of the current round of negotiations. We call upon Members to develop text for adoption. In so doing, Members shall consider proposals and the illustrative list of possible elements for Article VI:4 disciplines.[2]

**Approaches**

6. Pursuant to the principles and objectives above, we agree to intensify and expedite the request-offer negotiations, which shall remain the main method of negotiation, with a view to securing substantial commitments.

---

1 As attached to the Report by the Chairman to the Trade Negotiations Committee on 28 November 2005, contained in document TN/S/23. This attachment has no legal standing.

2 As attached to the Report of the Chairman of the Working Party on Domestic Regulation to the Special Session of the Council for Trade in Services on 15 November 2005, contained in document JOB(5)/280.

7. In addition to bilateral negotiations, we agree that the request-offer negotiations should also be pursued on a plurilateral basis in accordance with the principles of the GATS and the Guidelines and Procedures for the Negotiations on Trade in Services. The results of such negotiations shall be extended on an MFN basis. These negotiations would be organized in the following manner:

(a) Any Member or group of Members may present requests or collective requests to other Members in any specific sector or mode of supply, identifying their objectives for the negotiations in that sector or mode of supply.

(b) Members to whom such requests have been made shall consider such requests in accordance with paragraphs 2 and 4 of Article XIX of the GATS and paragraph 11 of the Guidelines and Procedures for the Negotiations on Trade in Services.

(c) Plurilateral negotiations should be organised with a view to facilitating the participation of all Members, taking into account the limited capacity of developing countries and smaller delegations to participate in such negotiations.

8. Due consideration shall be given to proposals on trade-related concerns of small economies.

9. Members, in the course of negotiations, shall develop methods for the full and effective implementation of the LDC Modalities, including expeditiously:

(a) Developing appropriate mechanisms for according special priority including to sectors and modes of supply of interest to LDCs in accordance with Article IV:3 of the GATS and paragraph 7 of the LDC Modalities.

(b) Undertaking commitments, to the extent possible, in such sectors and modes of supply identified, or to be identified, by LDCs that represent priority in their development policies in accordance with paragraphs 6 and 9 of the LDC Modalities.

(c) Assisting LDCs to enable them to identify sectors and modes of supply that represent development priorities.

(d) Providing targeted and effective technical assistance and capacity building for LDCs in accordance with the LDC Modalities, particularly paragraphs 8 and 12.

(e) Developing a reporting mechanism to facilitate the review requirement in paragraph 13 of the LDC Modalities.

10. Targeted technical assistance should be provided through, *inter alia*, the WTO Secretariat, with a view to enabling developing and least-developed countries to participate effectively in the negotiations. In particular and in accordance with paragraph 51 on Technical Cooperation of this Declaration, targeted technical assistance should be given to all developing countries allowing them to fully engage in the

negotiation. In addition, such assistance should be provided on, *inter alia*, compiling and analyzing statistical data on trade in services, assessing interests in and gains from services trade, building regulatory capacity, particularly on those services sectors where liberalization is being undertaken by developing countries.

**Timelines**

11. Recognizing that an effective timeline is necessary in order to achieve a successful conclusion of the negotiations, we agree that the negotiations shall adhere to the following dates:

(a) Any outstanding initial offers shall be submitted as soon as possible.

(b) Groups of Members presenting plurilateral requests to other Members should submit such requests by 28 February 2006 or as soon as possible thereafter.

(c) A second round of revised offers shall be submitted by 31 July 2006.

(d) Final draft schedules of commitments shall be submitted by 31 October 2006.

(e) Members shall strive to complete the requirements in 9(a) before the date in 11(c).

**Review of Progress**

12. The Special Session of the Council for Trade in Services shall review progress in the negotiations and monitor the implementation of the Objectives, Approaches and Timelines set out in this Annex.